The Whole Bowl

GLUTEN-FREE, DAIRY-FREE SOUPS & STEWS

The Whole Bowl
GLUTEN-FREE, DAIRY-FREE SOUPS & STEWS

The Countryman Press
Woodstock, VT
www.countrymanpress.com

Rebecca Wood & Leda Scheintaub

Book design and composition by Vicky Vaughn Shea, Ponderosa Pine Design

Photography by Beth Shepard Communications, LLC

Published by The Countryman Press, P.O. Box 748, Woodstock, VT 05091

Distributed by W. W. Norton & Company, Inc., 500 Fifth Avenue, New York, NY 10110

Printed in the United States of America

The Whole Bowl

978-1-58157-291-9

10 9 8 7 6 5 4 3 2 1

To Nash, my husband and stock-making partner

—LS

For the intention and well-being of

Dzigar Kongtrul Rinpoche

May all beings, as far as are the limits of the sky, be well nourished.

—RW

CONTENTS

Introduction:
I'M HUNGRY

People often ask me what motivated me to write *The New Whole Foods Encyclopedia*, the book I'm most known for. I might say that it goes back to the days on my grandparents' farm in Utah, where we ate with the seasons and made our bread, jams, and just about everything else from scratch. I might say it was because years back I was one of the first Westerners to write about the healing properties of whole foods and then-exotic grains, such as quinoa, Kamut, and teff. This all may be true, but the main reason I wrote the encyclopedia was that I was hungry. While I loved sharing important food wisdom and creating recipes, my underlying motivation was that I wanted everyone—myself included—to be well nourished. That's because I was never truly satisfied with what I ate—I grew up a long time before gluten and dairy sensitivities were on the radar, so it took years before I understood just why I was so hungry.

While I was growing up, Mom did all the cooking from scratch, meals cooked with love and care. But when everyone else was pleasantly full, I would still have the nibbles and be picking at the cookies while we cleaned up. This continued throughout my childhood and up into college—I was always hungry and constantly feeding what I would later realize were wheat and dairy cravings. I stayed hungry through various dietary forays, getting high on brown rice with the hippies in the late 1960s and studying macrobiotics with Michio Kushi in Boston. Getting cancer after twenty years of macrobiotics, I returned meat to my diet as part of my natural cure. I was still hungry while I wrote *The Splendid Grain*—working on this project, it was easy to convince myself that for professional reasons I had to keep eating wheat!

Finally, many meals and years away from my mother's table, I figured it out: I was gluten and dairy intolerant—that my intolerances had led to a whole host of symptoms, first and foremost an insatiable hunger. The other symptoms, including severe bloating, excruciatingly painful joints, bowel irregularity, and aphasia (the inability to remember words), had gotten so bad that I had no choice but to say good-bye to gluten in 1995 and, a few years later, to all dairy. And now that I've figured it out, today I delight in satisfying meals, even-keeled mental and physical energy, and being free of the munchies! It's my pleasure to help other people restore or maintain their health the gluten- and dairy-free way—and that's why it pleases me to offer this book.

While I was working on the second edition of *The New Whole Foods Encyclopedia*, I was living in a town in Colorado with a year-round population of fewer than three hundred people. My publishers were sophisticated New Yorkers; they were all cordial but down to business. At one point I was given the phone number of my book's managing editor, Leda Scheintaub. I remember my first, and a little nervous, call to Leda. I immediately felt at ease as she shared with me that just that morning she had made the Ginger Carrots and Hiziki recipe from my manuscript and she liked it! She was enthusiastic about my book, and I was just delighted. I soon asked her to edit articles for my website, www.RebeccaWood.com, and our friendship continues to blossom. She tells me that auspicious phone meeting—that glimpse into the world of traditional and medicinal foods and the possibility of taking her love for food to a deeper level—was her initial inspiration to enroll in cooking school and ultimately become a cookbook author herself.

Leda and I have feasted in each other's homes and over a burner that we backpacked deep into the Sangre de Cristo wilderness. We explore ideas and share cooking insights, and she challenges my culinary

Making Stock a Habit

Our book begins with three stock recipes, which are the basis for most of our soups and stews. While any of our recipes may be made with water, we invite you to consider a stock-making habit. A good stock can be the single most important ingredient in your soup, and the health benefits of homemade stock based on bones are immense (see page 5 to learn more), something you won't want to pass up on. Making your own is really more about organization than time, as a simmering pot of stock requires but minutes of actual preparation. You may substitute a prepared stock, but before you do so, taste it. Then reconsider. We're yet to find a commercial stock that truly enhances the flavor of good ingredients. And from an energetic vantage, a canned or shelf-stable product does not impart vigor, as do fresh whole foods.

If making your own stock seems a stretch, not to worry; we generously use ingredients high in umami flavor, such as mushrooms, tomatoes, fermented foods, kombu seaweed, and lard, which act as an "instant" stock by adding a noticeably hearty flavor. A bonus: Recipes that call for meat on the bone, such as our very first soup recipe, Easy Chicken Soup with Spinach and Dill (page 12), as well as Gulyás (page 96), Tamari and Toasted Sesame–Brushed Pork Rib Soup (page 38), Yucatán Turkey Thigh and Yucca Soup (page 68), Posole with Lamb (page 94), Congee (page 92), and Tibetan Thukpa (page 86), make their own stock as they cook.

assumptions. Leda has taken ownership of my whole food philosophy to share it with her generation. What an incalculable gift is that? In coauthoring our first book together we culled our personal favorite soup and stew recipes and then Leda managed the detailed process of turning them into a book. We share our profound wish for you to be nourished and satisfied and to delight in your kitchen creativity.

The Whole Bowl contains fifty great soup, stew, and accompaniment recipes to feed you throughout the year. It is about delighting in your daily food, and finding your way to good health as you do so. It's what fills the soup bowl every day of the gluten- and dairy-free week.

Some of the recipes have a targeted healing mission, such as the Cold Quell Soup (page 20), based on pungent congestion-busting mustard greens. Others are comfort food fare, such as Easy Chicken Soup with Spinach and Dill (page 12), Slow-Cooker Pork Tinga (page 84), and Cream of Mushroom Soup (page 44). A shared love for Asian food is evident, as in Tibetan Thukpa (page 86), Soba in a Basket (page 30), and

Mulligatawny Soup (page 58). Simple broth-based soups, such as Triple Fennel Soup (page 32) and Roasted Daikon Soup with Dandelion Greens and Hazelnut Oil (page 28), are joined by creamy soups, such as Leek and Scallion Soup with Garlic Cream (page 52), Carrot Soup with Garlic Chips (page 48), and Cultured White Gazpacho (page 43). Many of our recipes are meals in a bowl, such as Posole with Lamb (page 94) and Buffalo Chili (page 66), and others can easily be expanded into a meal with a few simple tweaks.

Our recipes reflect our commitment to health, healing, and good taste; all are made with real food: no ersatz ingredients to try to make you feel you're eating something you're not. They are not replacements for gluten- and dairy-containing dishes, as so many current books on the subject are; they are exceptional recipes in their own right that will please lovers of good food. There's something for everyone, from die-hard meat and potatoes people to ethnic food aficionados to the vegans among us. So pull up a spoon and dig in—soup's on!

—RW

STOCKS

Bone Stock

There's good reason why traditional chicken soup is fondly dubbed "Grandma's penicillin." Stock made of bones not only combats the flu by fortifying the immune system; it is also a classic protein-rich energy tonic that increases endurance. Bone stock also strengthens the gastrointestinal tract, veins, arteries, muscles, tendons, skin, and bones. Cooks worldwide and through the centuries have regarded silky, gelatinous bone stock as an essential ingredient for savory dishes.

How does purchased stock compare to homemade? Like cut glass to a diamond. Today's commercial gelatin is derived only from hides and skin; it is not an energy tonic. In contrast, gelatin extracted from bones is a nutritious source of protein as well as collagen, calcium, minerals, and the amino acids proline and glycine. Bone stock is a remarkably healing food.

The secret to a bone energy stock is long cooking with a little vinegar or wine—which act as a solvent—to extract nutrients. Because bones are dense, it takes a long time to draw out all their nutrients. Ideally chilled stock is thickly quivering like pudding and then clear again when you reheat it. A thin stock may result from too much water or too little cooking time; likewise, overcooking will break up the earliest-released gelatin molecule chains and produce (when chilled) a thin gelatin. But know that regardless of the outcome, your homemade stock will be a superfood!

As bone sizes and densities vary, use the cooking times as guidelines, and with repetition you'll soon be able to gauge the best cooking time for each batch. Also rely on your sense of smell to "tell" when it is done. It's fine to use different kinds of bones in the same batch; you can also use poultry skin. By adding flavoring agents, the stock's rich aroma whets the appetite. (The aroma of stock without seasonings is strong enough that one of our friends prepares hers in a slow cooker in the garage.) We add salt to our bone stock at the beginning

Stock for All Seasons

This stock is the nonvegetarian backbone of our soup and stew recipes, so it goes with any season and any soup preparation but the fish soups. In the winter you'll love how it warms your kitchen. Come summer, reach for a cooler option, the slow cooker (if you don't already have one, we highly recommend purchasing one—a basic model costs under twenty dollars) to make your stock, or consider using the quick-cooking Vegetable Stock (page 8) or Kombu-Shiitake Stock (page 9) on the hottest of hot days.

For a hot-weather stock, we don't use cloves and go lighter on the other warming spices, such as black mustard seeds, allspice, and garlic. In any season, you choose how much—if any—of the fat that typically rises to the top of the stock to use; fat not only makes a dish more satisfying, it also makes it more warming. While poultry fat (schmaltz) and pork fat (lard) lend exquisite flavor, sheep fat and beef fat (tallow) have a neutral flavor.

of cooking, as salt helps draw minerals from the bones and boosts the stock's flavor and shelf life. Depending on how much salt you add, reduce the amount of salt accordingly in the soup and stew recipes that follow.

We make a week's supply of this tonic stock and use it liberally in our soups, stews, and any savory dish that calls for liquid. Or, for a quick energy boost, we season it to taste and drink it as an on-the-spot restorative consommé.

MAKES ABOUT 3½ QUARTS STOCK

2	pounds raw or cooked bones (buffalo, beef, lamb, pork, poultry, or game)
4	quarts water
1	small whole onion, peeled
1	carrot
1	garlic clove, peeled
2	bay leaves, or 1 celery stalk with leaves
2	tablespoons traditionally aged vinegar or ½ cup wine (any type)
1 to 2	tablespoons spices of choice, such as allspice berries, chopped ginger, cardamom pods, coriander seeds, fennel seeds, cumin seeds, peppercorns, dried chiles, black mustard seeds, or a combination
1 or 2	whole cloves (optional)
	Unrefined salt

Place the bones and water in a 6- to 8-quart nonreactive stockpot. Bring to a boil over medium-high heat, then reduce the heat and simmer for 5 minutes with the lid off. Skim off and discard any foam (which is soluble protein) that rises to the surface. Add the onion, carrot, garlic, bay leaves, vinegar, and spices and season with salt. Return to a simmer, then reduce the heat to the lowest setting so the stock is at a bare simmer.

The cooking times are approximate, as extraction from larger bones and/or older animals takes longer than extraction from smaller bones and/or younger animals.

Beef bones—simmer for 8 to 10 hours (pressure-cook for 2 hours, or cook in a slow cooker for 24 hours).

Pork and lamb—simmer for 3 hours (pressure-cook for 1½ hours, or cook in a slow cooker for 18 hours).

Poultry bones—simmer for 2 hours (pressure-cook for 1 hour, or cook in a slow cooker for 6 to 12 hours).

Top of the Morning

Just as we wouldn't start a long trip with an empty tank of gas, so we need nurture at the start of the day. And that's why historically throughout the world, people have greeted the new day by breaking fast with a substantial breakfast. Traditional Chinese Medicine regards a good breakfast eaten within three hours of rising as a requisite to health. We know elderly and convalescing Asians who religiously drink bone stock both as their first morning beverage and as an afternoon restorative.

If for whatever reason you skimp on breakfast, consider reaching for a cup of Bone Stock as an energy tonic. Add some ginger or a pinch of salt, or even steep a bag of green or black tea into it. It's surprisingly tasty and deeply satisfying. And while it's not a true meal replacement, it's sure to give more gusto than many of the typical packaged meal replacements on the market.

When the stock is cool enough to work with, strain through a fine-mesh strainer lined with a layer of cheesecloth, reserving all but the dregs. (Optional: Reuse the bones by adding fresh water, vinegar, and seasoning agents and cook for a second or third extraction. Or let the bones cool and freeze them to make another round at a later time.)

Refrigerate the stock, tightly covered, for up to 1 week, or freeze for up to 3 months. To use the stock immediately, remove any excess fat. Season with salt to taste and seasonings of choice and drink hot, or use in soups, sauces, and grain dishes, anywhere stock is called for.

VARIATIONS

Add meat scraps, raw or cooked, to heighten flavor and nutrition.
Roast the bones until browned for increased flavor before making your stock.

Vegetable Stock

This vegetarian stock involves very little active time, saves you money over store-bought, and adds depth to any soup or stew you include it in, outperforming the best of bouillon cubes, cans, or boxes. Here the vegetables are sautéed to extract extra flavor, but when time is tight or you want the clearest of stocks, skip that step (you might also skip the kombu, as along with its abundant minerals it adds a slight tint of green to the liquid), add all the ingredients to the pot, and cook as directed.

For impromptu stock making, save vegetable scraps (just about anything goes, except cabbage family members; onion and garlic skins are flavorful additions, as are corn cobs and pea pods) in a plastic bag or container in the refrigerator or freezer; when there's enough to fill a pot halfway, toss them all in, add a piece of kombu and some salt, pour in water to cover, and proceed as directed.

MAKES 4 QUARTS STOCK

2	tablespoons extra-virgin olive oil		2	bay leaves
2	large onions, chopped		1	(3- to 4-inch) piece kombu seaweed
3	large carrots, chopped			Unrefined salt
2	large celery stalks, including leaves, chopped		1	teaspoon black peppercorns
4	garlic cloves, smashed (include the peels)		4	quarts water
2	handfuls fresh parsley or cilantro stems or sprigs			

Heat the oil in a large stockpot over medium heat. Add the onions, carrots, celery, and garlic and cook, stirring frequently, until well browned, about 10 minutes. Add the remaining ingredients, including salt to taste, and bring to a boil. Reduce the heat to very low, cover, and cook at a bare simmer for 45 minutes. Strain the broth through a fine-mesh strainer into a heatproof bowl. Use immediately, or let cool, pour into containers, and store in the refrigerator for up to 1 week or the freezer for up to 3 months.

Kombu-Shiitake Stock

This uplifting stock is a version of the classic Japanese kombu stock, also known as dashi, heightened with dried shiitake mushrooms to double the umami—earthy—flavor. It enhances any savory dish and is also delicious on its own. An alternative to seasoning with salt is to include a little wheat-free tamari for an authentic Japanese flavor. Make an ample supply and keep refrigerated until ready to use; it will keep for up to 1 week.

MAKES ABOUT 7 CUPS STOCK

1	(6- to 8-inch) strip kombu seaweed
3 or 4	dried shiitake mushrooms
7	cups water
	Unrefined salt

Place the kombu, mushrooms, water, and salt to taste in a large saucepan and soak for at least 15 minutes or as long as 10 hours.

Place the pan over medium-high heat and bring to a simmer. Reduce the heat and simmer for 5 to 10 minutes, then remove the kombu and reserve it for another use, such as another soup, a stew, or a braised vegetable dish, or discard it. Continue to simmer for an additional 5 to 10 minutes, until the mushrooms are softened. Remove the mushrooms and reserve them for another use; you could slice them and add to a soup or stir-fry, for example.

Kombu and Shiitake Mushrooms: A Detoxifying Duo

The word *detox* is often equated with cleaning out by fasting; we follow the Traditional Chinese Medicine way of using ingredients that both strengthen and gently detoxify. And two of the best foods for the purpose are kombu and shiitake mushrooms.

Both shiitake mushrooms and kombu—a sea vegetable—have remarkable medicinal properties: Shiitake is a blood and *qi* tonic (meaning it gently builds and enhances overall vital energy) that detoxifies and reduces inflammation, has antiviral properties, and boosts the immune system; kombu is also a blood and *qi* tonic and strengthens the nervous system, adrenals, bones, and teeth, and helps remove toxins from the body, including radioactive contaminants.

So make this kombu- and shiitake-rich stock and use it liberally in the soup recipes that follow. Or for an on-the-spot pick-me-up, add a little grated fresh ginger, garnish with scallion slices, and bottoms up!

Seaweed and Radiation

Given the increasing concern about radiation contamination of ocean fish, one is wise to query if the same might be true for seaweed. And here's excellent news: Many natural food suppliers (both large companies and cottage crafters) are posting online the chemical and radiation assay reports provided by independent laboratories, and their results show no heavy metal or radioactive isotope contamination of their products. Would that all food producers provide such careful documentation regarding the quality of their goods. Consider checking out various suppliers' web pages and shop accordingly.

BROTHY SOUPS

Easy Chicken Soup with Spinach and Dill

This powerful soup is a nutrient-dense energy tonic, a delicious prescription. What is the difference between another chicken soup and this medicinal recipe? The secret is using a whole chicken to make the soup stock, rather than opening up a box of prepared stock and throwing in some chicken parts, a shortcut you'll find in many recipes. Then long simmering—similar to the method you'll find in our Bone Stock (page 5)—extracts invaluable nutrients, collagen, and flavor from the chicken carcass. And the yam gives a wonderful color, flavor, and texture to the soup.

While this recipe is universal to all seasons and places, you may want to adjust it with the weather: in the colder months, try upping the amount of garlic, ginger, and chiles to increase circulation and promote warmth, and consider reducing them during the summer. And for lighter summer fare, consider replacing the yam with 1 large, chopped zucchini; add it during the last five minutes of cooking.

SERVES 6 TO 8

1	(4- to 5-pound) organic chicken, washed, or 5 pounds of chicken pieces with bones and skin
1	tablespoon minced fresh ginger
2	garlic cloves, minced
1	teaspoon ground cumin
2	bay leaves
	Unrefined salt and freshly ground black pepper
1	large yam, peeled and cubed
1	large onion, chopped
1	jalapeño chile, seeded and chopped
2	celery stalks, including leaves, chopped
2	cups baby spinach leaves
½	cup chopped fresh dill

Place the chicken breast side up in a large pot and add water to just cover. Place over high heat, bring to a boil, then reduce the heat and simmer uncovered for 10 minutes. Do not boil. Skim off and discard the foam that rises to the top. Add the ginger, garlic, cumin, bay leaves, and salt and pepper to taste. Return to a simmer, partially cover, and simmer for about 45 minutes, until the breast meat is cooked through.

Carefully lift out the chicken, using a slotted spoon or tongs, and place on a large plate. Pull the breast meat from the chicken, using tongs and a fork, and reserve the breast meat on the plate. Return the rest of the chicken to the pot and cook for 30 minutes, then again carefully lift the chicken from the pot, using tongs and a fork, and place on another large plate. Let cool enough that you can comfortably handle it, then pick the meat off the bones and tear it into bite-size pieces. Return the dark meat to the pot, add the yam, onion, jalapeño, and celery, and simmer for an additional 20 minutes, or until the vegetables are softened. Tear the breast meat into bite-size pieces and add it to the pot.

Stir in the spinach and simmer for about 1 minute, until it wilts. Adjust the seasoning with salt and pepper, stir in the dill, and serve.

Thai-Style Turkey Meatball Noodle Soup

ost traditional meatball recipes contain both wheat, in the form of bread crumbs, and dairy, often Parmesan cheese. We're happy to report that neither is essential to a great meatball: they aren't needed to hold the meatballs together, and without them, no fillers or binders get between you and the meat.

This simple meatball, seasoned with a blend of herbs and spices, is simmered in a soup base featuring the Thai trinity of fish sauce, lime juice, and chiles, all of which we recommend keeping on hand at all times for impromptu Asian-style soup making. The fish sauce and chile-garlic sauce are available in Asian grocery stores.

Feel free to double the quantity of the meatballs and freeze them for up to two months; drop them into a pot of simmering stock to cook through and you've got a simple meal solution. You can make the meatballs with chicken, beef, or pork in place of the turkey, if you like.

SERVES 4 AS A STARTER OR 2 AS A MEAL

MEATBALLS

1	pound ground organic turkey, preferably dark meat
¼	medium onion, minced
2	garlic cloves, pressed through a garlic press
¼	cup minced fresh cilantro leaves
¼	cup minced fresh mint
1	small green chile, minced
½	teaspoon unrefined salt

SOUP BASE

6	cups stock (pages 5–10)
1	tablespoon chile-garlic sauce, plus more for serving
1	bundle (about 4 ounces total) bean thread noodles (see sidebar, page 26), soaked and cut into pieces
¼	cup Asian fish sauce, plus more for serving
¼	cup fresh lime juice
	Chopped fresh cilantro, for garnish

Make the turkey meatballs: In a large bowl, combine all the ingredients and mix very well to incorporate. Form the mixture into about twenty 1½-inch balls. Place on a plate and set aside.

Make the soup base: Heat the stock in a large saucepan over high heat. Add the chile-garlic sauce. Using a slotted spoon, carefully add the meatballs to the stock. Bring to a simmer, then reduce the heat to low, cover, and simmer for 15 minutes.

Add the noodles and cook until they're transparent, from 30 seconds to several minutes depending upon the variety, then add the fish sauce and lime juice. Spoon into bowls and top each bowl with cilantro and mint. Pass the chile-garlic sauce and fish sauce at the table.

Not Just Cold-Weather Fare

We tend to think of noodle soup as cold-weather fare, a go-to food for cold and flu season, but in Asian countries steamy, meat-based, brothy soups are enjoyed regardless of the temperature outside. To make the soup more summery, try doubling up on the mint; or in the winter, omitting it. An extra chile or two makes it more warming for the winter, as would the addition of hearty winter greens, such as kale or collards.

Pepper Water with Beef

It's a soup, but you serve it on a plate and you eat it with your fingers.

Pepper water, also known as *rassam*, is an Anglo-Indian soup made with tomatoes, tamarind, chiles, and lots of peppercorns. It's not the simplest recipe in this book, but it's worth the effort when you have the time for something a little different. The trick to finishing this dish is in what Indians call tempering, a process in which spices are added one at a time to hot oil to bring out their flavors; the spice oil is poured into the soup at the end and infuses the dish with flavor. Cooking the pepper water soup base alone is another, quicker option—the peppery, garlicky broth makes a nice winter starter soup. Tamarind, ginger-garlic paste, and curry leaves are available at Indian grocery stores (you can make your own ginger-garlic paste by mincing equal amounts of garlic and ginger by weight in a food processor). If you can't find curry leaves, it's fine to omit them.

Leda's husband, Nash Patel, who is Anglo-Indian, grew up with this recipe and turned our concept of soup upside down with it. To have a go, put a good scoop of rice on a rimmed plate, pour the soup on top, finish the plate with a spoonful of beef, and dig in.

SERVES 4 AS A STARTER OR 2 AS A MEAL

PEPPER WATER

2½ cups water or stock (pages 5–10)	½ teaspoon ground cumin
1 teaspoon tamarind concentrate, dissolved in 1 tablespoon hot water	¼ teaspoon ground black mustard seeds
3 large tomatoes, chopped	½ teaspoon ground coriander
7 unpeeled garlic cloves, smashed	½ teaspoon freshly ground black pepper, or to taste
10 sprigs fresh cilantro	¼ teaspoon cayenne pepper
4 fresh curry leaves (optional)	¼ teaspoon ground turmeric
	1 teaspoon unrefined salt, or to taste

BEEF

1	pound pastured stewing beef, cut into 2-inch pieces
1	red onion, cut into half-rings
1	cup water
½	teaspoon unrefined salt, plus more to taste
¼	teaspoon cayenne pepper

¼	teaspoon ground turmeric
2	tablespoons extra-virgin olive oil
1½	teaspoons ginger-garlic paste
1	teaspoon ground cumin
¼	teaspoon ground black mustard seeds

TEMPERING FOR THE PEPPER WATER

2	tablespoons extra-virgin olive oil
½	teaspoon black mustard seeds
½	teaspoon cumin seeds
4	garlic cloves, smashed, with skin left on

1 to 3	dried red chiles, to taste
1	sprig fresh curry leaves
	White rice, for serving

Make the pepper water: In a medium saucepan, combine all the ingredients. Place over high heat and bring to a boil. Reduce the heat to low, cover, and cook for 30 minutes, mashing the tomatoes two or three times with a potato masher or the back of a wooden spoon, to release all the juices. Strain through a fine-mesh strainer into a heatproof bowl, pressing on the solids to extract all the flavorful liquid. Taste and add more salt if needed.

While the pepper water is cooking, make the beef: Combine the beef, onion, water, salt, cayenne, and turmeric in a large saucepan. Place over medium-high heat and bring to a boil, then reduce the heat to medium-low, cover, and cook for 40 minutes. Strain the beef mixture, reserving the juices.

Heat the oil in a large nonstick pan over medium heat. Add the ginger-garlic paste and cook, stirring, for 1 minute. Add the cumin and mustard seeds and cook for 30 seconds. Add the beef mixture and cook, stirring, for about 15 minutes, until nicely browned. Add about 1 cup of the reserved juices that you cooked the beef in (discard the rest) and scrape up the browned bits from the bottom of the pan; cook for about 5 minutes, until the beef has absorbed almost all of the liquid and you are left with a little bit of thick curry with the beef. Season with salt to taste.

Prepare the tempering for the pepper water: Rinse out the pan that you cooked the pepper water in. Pour in the oil and heat over medium-high heat. Add the mustard seeds and cumin seeds and cook, stirring, for about 1 minute, until the mustard seeds start to pop. Add the garlic, chiles, and curry leaves and cook, stirring, until the ingredients are nice and dark, just bordering on burnt, 4 to 5 minutes (pushing the boundary between sautéed and burnt is an important flavoring step). Add a little of the pepper water to the pot and stir, giving some distance between you and the pan so you don't get hit by the sputtering ingredients. Add the rest of the pepper water, bring to a boil, then reduce the heat and simmer for 3 minutes to combine the flavors. Taste and add more salt if needed. Strain out the garlic, chiles, and curry leaves, or leave them in for the effect (but warn diners not to eat the chiles).

To serve: Scoop some rice over rimmed plates. Pour some pepper water over the rice and spoon the beef onto the side of the plates. Mix everything together with your hands and serve, no spoon required. As you're eating, you may replenish your plate with additional pepper water to moisten the rice.

Choosing Quality Meat and Poultry

Take the time to inform yourself about the meat and chicken that goes into your soups and stews and favor pastured meat and organic poultry whenever you can. The main differences between quality and conventional meats are found in the foods the animals are fed and the manner in which the animals are raised. Children and pregnant women can especially benefit from avoiding conventional animal foods.

Organic animal feed is free of synthetic fertilizers, pesticides, herbicides, animal by-products, sewage sludge, antibiotics, and hormones; it cannot contain preservatives, additives, or GMOs. The predominant diet of conventional livestock is corn, soy, and wheat that often includes these unnatural substances.

We encourage you to ask your butcher about his or her suppliers or visit the producer's web page to post your query directly. Quality food ranchers gladly respond to customer questions. After all, they've proudly gone the extra mile to deliver quality and they know that an informed customer is most likely a return customer.

Organic Poultry: Animals can only be fed 100 percent organic feed (one that is predominantly soy, corn, and/or wheat) and free of antibiotics; they are allowed freedom of movement rather than being confined in tiny cubicles.

Pastured Beef, Buffalo, Pork, and Lamb: While the term *pastured meat* is not certified by the USDA, it is the one indicator that tells you the meat came from an animal that was raised outdoors on actively managed pasture, using the techniques of rotational grazing on nutrient-dense forage crops. These animals are treated humanely and ethically and not caged in tiny coops or otherwise tightly confined. Pastured animals may be fed some grain as a supplement to their grass-based diet, especially in the winter when it is harder to meet nutritional needs through hay and silage.

Grass-fed: Animals must eat only forage grasses after they are weaned; they may never be fed any grain or grain products. During the growing months, this can come from outdoor pastures; in the winter, animals may eat hay, silage, or other crop residues as long as they do not contain grain.

Grain-finished: Cattle, buffalo, and lamb are often "finished" (brought to full weight) on grain to help the animals gain weight and to increase the meat's juiciness, tenderness, and marbling.

Hormone-Free: Organic beef, buffalo, pork, and lamb will be hormone-free, with the producer providing documentation to support this claim (by law, poultry cannot contain hormones).

Cold Quell Soup

As their pungent bite indicates, mustard greens help move stuck energy. Think of sipping this soup as multitasking: While you're enjoying it, you're also moving pathogens out of your system!

Serve this bold yet simple soup at the first suggestion of a cold or flu as a bit of preventative medicine: The oil from the mustard greens warms the nasal passages, helps disperse congestion, and increases energy flow throughout the body, and the yam and ginger support *qi* and blood circulation. The sweet yam flavor acts as a counterpoint to the piquant greens and ginger.

In Asia this soup is considered most medicinal in the fall, but whenever you feel a cold coming on, you can turn to it as a pot of soothing relief. To double its nurturing whammy, use homemade bone stock (page 5). To turn the soup into a one-dish meal, add a protein such as chicken breast, or poach eggs in the simmering stock.

Note that if the greens are overcooked, they'll develop a strong cabbagelike aroma and turn a drab green color; and if they're undercooked, they'll be fiery hot. Getting them just right is easy: Simply simmer until their vibrant green deepens by several shades and they've lost enough of their bite to suit your palate.

SERVES 4

1	large yam, peeled and chopped
6	cups stock (pages 5–10) or water
1	tablespoon peeled and minced fresh ginger
1½	teaspoons unrefined salt, or to taste
1	bunch mustard greens, stems removed and leaves chopped
	Extra-virgin olive oil

Combine the yam, stock, ginger, and salt in a medium saucepan; place over medium-high heat and bring to a simmer. Cover, reduce the heat, and simmer for 15 minutes, or until the yam softens.

Add the mustard greens and simmer for 5 minutes, or until the greens are wilted and their color darkens a bit. Taste; your soup is done when the bite of the greens mellows to your liking. Adjust the seasonings, spoon into bowls, finish with a splash of oil, and serve.

Sticky Soup with Beef and Snow Pea Leaves

Early spring is the short window for snow pea leaves in southern Vermont, where Leda recently moved after a lifetime in New York City; these shoots from the snow pea plant are slightly sweet and fresh tasting and one of her most anticipated greens of the season. This soup was created to celebrate the richness of the New England harvest and to satisfy her passion for flavorful Asian food.

Don't miss out on this soup if snow pea season has passed; you can substitute watercress or thinly sliced spinach leaves, also with tasty results. Tapioca has become a key ingredient in gluten-free cooking and baking; now you can enjoy it—in the form of these sticky, toothsome pearls—in your soup as well.

If you've got stock on hand, the soup is easy to make; you can assemble the ingredients for the soup in the soup bowls while the tapioca is cooking, then just pour and serve. You can find large tapioca pearls in Asian and international food stores.

SERVES 4

5	tablespoons large white tapioca pearls			Cayenne pepper
4	ounces pastured sirloin, flank, rib eye, or other steak		2	cups snow pea leaves (if unavailable, substitute watercress or thinly sliced spinach)
5	cups stock (pages 5–10)		1	lime, cut into 4 wedges
1½	tablespoons tamari		2	scallions, thinly sliced
1	tablespoon unrefined brown sugar or palm sugar		¼	cup chopped fresh cilantro
	Unrefined salt			Garlic Chips (page 49; optional)

Bring a medium saucepan of water to a boil. Add the tapioca pearls, return to a boil, then reduce the heat and simmer for about 50 minutes, until the pearls are almost completely translucent with a small dot of white in the middle. Drain.

While the tapioca is cooking, place the beef in the freezer for about 15 minutes (freezing it makes it easier to slice), then slice it thinly against the grain.

Meanwhile, in a large saucepan, bring the stock to a boil. Stir in the tamari and brown sugar. Taste and season with salt and cayenne. Add the tapioca pearls.

Just before pouring the soup, divide the beef among the bowls. Increase the heat under the soup and bring it to a rolling boil; immediately pour the soup over the beef and stir to evenly cook the meat (pastured beef tends to get tough quickly; cooking as little as possible helps avoid this). Stir the snow pea leaves into the bowls until they are wilted. Squeeze the lime wedges over the soup and top with the scallions, cilantro, and garlic chips, if using. Serve immediately.

Soy Sauce Versus Tamari

For those of us avoiding wheat, we need to become expert label readers, as wheat makes its way into a host of unlikely foods, particularly packaged foods. To keep this recipe completely gluten free, you'll need to use tamari rather than soy sauce, as soy sauce contains a small amount of wheat; tamari is wheat free.

Vegetarian Tom Yum–Style Soup

The mission in making this soup was to give it an authentic Thai taste without using fish sauce, one of the key ingredients in Thai cuisine. So the focus was on the stock: intensely flavored, with tamarind and lots of citrus and Kaffir lime leaves to bring out the sour taste. The vegetables for the soup are cut very thinly and the soup is poured over them at the end to "cook" them while keeping them crisp. This soup was part of Leda's culinary school final project, dinner for a hundred people at the Natural Gourmet Institute in New York City.

If you want to get a little fancy, as Leda did for her dinner project, make the bird's nest topping—it's exciting to see the noodles puff up like a nest when they hit the oil. Who knew going gluten free could be this much fun?

SERVES 6 TO 8

SOUP BASE

1	large onion, cut into chunks	¼	cup tamari
4	large carrots, cut into chunks	8	Kaffir lime leaves (see sidebar)
4	celery stalks, including leaves	5	dried red chiles
1	(3-inch) piece fresh ginger	1	tablespoon tamarind concentrate
4	garlic cloves, peeled and smashed with the side of a knife	1	tablespoon pure maple syrup, or to taste
4	lemongrass stalks, cut into chunks and bruised with the side of a knife or a rolling pin		Unrefined salt (optional)
		10	cups water
1	bunch fresh cilantro		Juice of 1 lime, or to taste

Kaffir Lime Leaves

The Kaffir lime is a small, bumpy-looking lime grown in Southeast Asia. The leaves of the fruit are incredibly aromatic and they give a distinctive flavor to the food of that region. You can find Kaffir lime leaves in Asian grocery stores. If fresh are unavailable, frozen are a good substitute; dried leaves have lost much of their flavor.

BIRD'S NEST TOPPING (OPTIONAL)

Virgin coconut or red palm oil (these fats safely withstand high temperatures)

6 to 8   handfuls of rice vermicelli

Unrefined salt

SOUP TOPPING OPTIONS

Thinly sliced shiitake mushrooms and water chestnuts

Jicama, carrots, snow peas, and bell peppers, cut into julienne

Thai or regular basil leaves, cut into chiffonade (see page 85)

Make the soup base: In a large saucepan or stockpot, combine all the ingredients except the lime juice. Bring to a boil, then reduce the heat, cover loosely, and simmer for 1 hour. Strain the soup base into a large bowl and return to the pan.

Make the bird's nest topping, if using: While the soup base is cooking, line a baking sheet with paper towels. Heat about 3 inches of oil in a wok over high heat until very hot but not smoking. Put a handful of noodles in a spider (a wide, shallow wire-mesh basket with a long handle) or strainer and lower the noodles into the oil. The noodles will puff up in about 5 seconds. As soon as this happens, remove them from the oil, place on the prepared baking sheet, and sprinkle with salt.

Divide your choice of soup toppings among serving bowls, reserving the basil. Return the soup base to a boil and immediately pour the soup over the vegetables to wilt them. Add the basil, if using. Top with the bird's nests, if using, and serve immediately.

Gluten-Free Pasta Options

While some gluten-free pasta is great, there's plenty that's not. Here's how to discern between the two extremes before the noodles land in your pot. Note: If you're new to gluten-free pasta, don't expect it to taste or perform like traditional semolina pasta. Follow the directions given on the package, as cooking instructions vary depending on what they're made from.

Pasta with Precedent: If a pasta variety has been used for centuries, trust that there are good culinary reasons for its continued presence. Two grain-based pastas—those made from 100 percent buckwheat or rice—fall under this category, as do noodles made from various starchy vegetables, which become transparent when cooked. These are known as glass noodles, cellophane noodles, Chinese vermicelli, or bean thread noodles. These noodles may also be made from mung bean starch, canna, cassava, yam (konjac), or kudzu. In some cases they may be flavored with other ingredients, such as acorns in Korea or mugwort, green tea, and lotus in Japan. While each has its own personality, their texture ranges from light and almost airy (bean threads) to even more substantial than whole-grain pasta (kudzu).

100% Grain Pasta: Any nongluten grain may be extruded into pasta. The most common grain-based, gluten-free pastas are made from quinoa, rice, corn, and buckwheat. Less commonly available grain pastas include those made from millet, oats, sorghum, and wild rice. Depending upon the brand, gluten-free grain pastas vary considerably in quality.

Seaweed Pasta: What's simply great about versatile seaweed pasta is that it may be cooked right into a soup for fifteen minutes or more and, unlike any other pasta—gluten free or otherwise—retain its shape. And if you think you might not like the taste of seaweed, not to worry—seaweed pasta doesn't taste fishy; depending upon the variety it has either a mild flavor or no flavor of its own. Seaweed is a true superfood in both nutritional profile and ability to chelate heavy metals and radioactive toxins.

Given the diversity of the sea garden, it's not surprising that there's a long, skinny seaweed called sea spaghetti (*Himanthalia elongata*) that looks like—and cooks up like—noodles. This brown algae, harvested from the Baltic Sea, North Sea, and northeast Atlantic Ocean, has a pleasing and mild flavor that's reminiscent of asparagus. Sea spaghetti is available online from several cottage crafters.

Kelp noodles, a traditional Korean food, are also extracted from brown algae, and multiple brands are available. One made-in-the-USA brand is Sea Tangle; it imparts no flavor of its own and readily absorbs the flavors of the foods it's cooked with.

Mung Bean Pasta (aka Cellophane Noodles, Bean Threads, Glass Noodles): Pasta made from mung bean starch is a traditional pasta choice, and it's readily digestible. Carefully read the ingredients list and purchase only those containing mung bean starch (sometimes listed as pea starch), as some varieties may be cut with an unidentified starch.

Pasta Containing Other Bean Flours or Starches (Don't Do It!): It's with good reason that using raw bean flour as an ingredient was largely unprecedented until, in an attempt to boost protein, soy flour was added to various products in the 1960s (minor exceptions include the toasted chickpea flour used in some Indian dishes and the roasted black soy flour that makes its way into Japanese dishes). Bean flour is notoriously more difficult to digest than are beans themselves (during the normal soaking and cooking of beans, many of their antinutrients are removed). Bypass pasta that includes the flour from soybeans, black beans, lupine, or other legumes.

Tapioca Noodles: This translucent and chewy noodle made from tapioca, sometimes mixed with rice flour, is featured in Chinese, Vietnamese, and Cambodian cuisine. This noodle has virtually no flavor of its own and takes on the flavors of the dish it's cooked into.

Potato Starch: A small amount of potato starch may be used as filler in some gluten-free pasta.

Cooking Gluten-Free Pasta

When using any gluten-free grain pasta, it's critical to cook it in abundant water. Add 8 ounces of pasta to 2½ quarts of vigorously boiling salted water and include a tablespoon of olive oil to prevent it from sticking. If less water is used, the pasta stews rather than boils, which results in a gummy texture.

Nongrain pasta is often added to tepid water to cover, and with seaweed pasta, the temperature of the cooking liquid is not important—it may be added to boiling or cold water.

Roasted Daikon Soup with Dandelion Greens and Hazelnut Oil

While all raw radishes tend to have a bite, daikon is particularly pungent. Roasting so transforms its bite and bitter note into an earthy sweetness that turning on the oven to roast a chicken or bake a cake is an invitation to roast a daikon as well. But if there's nothing else to fill the oven, conserve energy by baking the daikon in your toaster oven. And, if you wish, bake it a day in advance, as once the daikon is cooked and the greens are at hand, putting this soup together is a snap. The drizzle of hazelnut oil makes a fine finish.

While the dandelion greens found year round at the greengrocers work well in this soup, for a special springtime delicacy, we encourage you to forage dandelions so that you can feast on their crowns and buds (see sidebar).

Early spring dandelions are sweeter than leaves from a plant that has blossomed and set seed. In the fall, the leaves are again less bitter than in midseason. Cultivated dandelion greens from the store are less bitter than the wild ones, but in both cases you'll want to nibble on a leaf to ascertain its tang and gauge how much to include in your dish. If the taste is too bitter for your liking, parboiling resolves this. By the way, dandelions are among the healthiest of greens.

So people can adjust the soup to their taste, serve with lemon as sour (in addition to the sweet, pungent, and salty tastes already contained in this soup) moderates the bitterness.

SERVES 4

1	large daikon (about 12 inches long)	4	scallions, white and green parts, chopped
6	cups stock (pages 5–10)		Freshly ground black pepper
1	teaspoon unrefined salt, or to taste		Unrefined hazelnut or extra-virgin olive oil
8	ounces dandelion greens (about 4 cups), chopped	4	lemon slices

Preheat the oven to 350°F.

Place the whole daikon on a baking sheet and roast for 1 hour, or until softened but still firm. Remove from the oven and let cool. Peel and discard the skin, then dice the daikon.

Place the daikon in a large saucepan and add the stock and salt. Place over medium-high heat and bring to a boil. Add the dandelion greens, cover, reduce the heat, and simmer for 5 minutes. Add the scallions and season with pepper to taste; taste and adjust the salt as needed.

Spoon into bowls, drizzle with oil, and serve each bowl with a slice of lemon.

Jeweled Dandelion Crowns

Dandelion crowns are a treat that money can't buy; in texture, color, and taste they're reminiscent of the base or heart of a head of celery, with only a light dandelion essence. Adorning the crownlike jewels are its pearl-size nascent buds, which make a creamy smooth nibble. Once the buds become as large as a thumbnail, they're less toothsome and so not used.

When spring comes, watch closely, and as dandelions start setting leaf but before their characteristic yellow blossoms appear, grab a small paring knife or a sturdy spoon and forage. Find a cluster of dandelion greens and carve a cone-shaped piece of crown right from the center of their leafy rosette, leaving the root (and most of the dirt) still in the ground.

Slice the crown, add it to your soup, and simmer until tender. Then add the buds along with the greens. Be forewarned: Once you try dandelion crowns and buds, odds are you'll have acquired a new springtime ritual.

Soba in a Basket (Zaru Soba)

On a sizzling summer day when the heat so drains your energy that you can't imagine having supper, here's a traditional soba (Japanese buckwheat noodle) dish guaranteed to both whet your appetite and revive you. Look for 100 percent gluten-free soba made with only buckwheat; though it is more delicate than your average buckwheat soba, which is cut with wheat, it's worth the extra care for its unadulterated flavor.

Place the basket of just cooked soba and a variety of condiments with small serving spoons at the table. At each place setting arrange two small (about pint-size) bowls, one empty and the second filled halfway with the dipping sauce. This sauce may be made a day or so in advance; use the best-quality tamari soy sauce available, ideally one that has been traditionally brewed and aged in cedar casks for two years.

Each person places into an empty bowl pinches of his or her condiments of choice, then with chopsticks takes a portion of the soba, gives it a quick dunk into their dipping sauce, then dips it into the condiment bowl and eats it. To retain the delicate flavor of the soba, select just a smattering of condiments and don't allow the soba to rest in the dipping sauce. At meal's end, pour some of the reserved soba cooking water into each person's remaining dipping sauce as a brothy palate cleanser.

If you wish to expedite this dish, you can bypass the basket and individual condiment bowls; simply divide the cooked soba into four bowls, add condiments, and serve with individual bowls of the dipping sauce.

SERVES 4

DIPPING SAUCE (MAKES ABOUT 3 CUPS)

⅓	cup traditionally aged mirin (sweet rice cooking wine)
2	cups traditionally aged tamari
¾	cup Kombu-Shiitake Stock (page 9)
1 to 2	tablespoons unrefined cane sugar

SOBA

1 (8.8-ounce) package 100% buckwheat soba

4 scallions, thinly sliced on the diagonal

2 sheets nori seaweed, folded into eighths and cut into 2 x ¼–inch strips

¼ cup dried bonito (Japanese fish flakes)

2 tablespoons powdered and reconstituted wasabi or grated fresh ginger

¼ cup toasted sesame seeds

Make the dipping sauce: Place the mirin in a small saucepan, bring to a boil to evaporate the alcohol, and immediately reduce the heat to low. Add the tamari, stock, and sugar and bring to a bare simmer; do not let it boil. Stir to dissolve the sugar. Taste, and if necessary, mellow the flavor by adding more stock or sugar, with the goal of a robustly flavored dipping sauce. If a cloudy foam accumulates on the top, skim it off. The sauce can be used immediately, but it is better the next day. Refrigerated it will last a week.

Make the soba: Cook the soba (see sidebar), reserving some of the cooking water for an end of the meal "soup" that will be combined with the remaining dipping sauce. Gently place the soba in a food-grade basket or on a sushi mat resting atop a plate for serving.

Place the scallions, nori, bonito, wasabi, and sesame seeds into separate condiment bowls. Serve as described in the headnote, with individual bowls of the dipping sauce and an empty bowl to hold portions of the condiments of choice along with just-dipped strands of soba. At the meal's end, pour the reserved cooking water into the dipping sauce bowls and drink as a digestif.

How to Cook Soba Noodles

Have ready a large bowl filled with cold water to plunge the cooked soba into.

Pour 2 quarts water into a 4-quart saucepan, add 1 teaspoon of salt, and bring to a boil. Grab approximately one third of the soba, fan it out (to prevent it from clumping together in the pot), and drop it in the water. Quickly repeat with the remaining one-third portions and stir gently to immerse them all in the water. Return the water to a gentle boil, then reduce the heat to a low boiling point. When the water threatens to boil over, "shock" the noodles by adding about ½ cup of cold water; repeat the shocking process as necessary and cook for 7 to 8 minutes, or as indicated on the package directions, as some varieties are thinner than others. Watch closely, as overcooked soba turns mushy. Taste a strand, and the instant it is cooked through, strain out the cooking water; with 100 percent buckwheat soba, err on the side of undercooked. Plunge the cooked soba into the cold water. Gently swirl the soba around to cool it; once this water becomes tepid, gently drain it off, and carefully pour in additional cold water. Rinse thoroughly and drain.

Triple Fennel Soup

Fennel lovers, this one is for you! Fennel bulb, seeds, and feathery fronds join forces in this light starter soup; to further the effect, garnish the soup with a little shaved raw fennel. The soup's lemony finish can be enhanced by topping with a scattering of finely chopped salt-preserved lemon (see page 56).

To add a warming element to the soup, stir in a little fresh ginger juice at the end. Save the fennel stalks and cores for soup stock.

SERVES 4

2 tablespoons extra-virgin olive oil, plus more for drizzling	2 garlic cloves, chopped
4 shallots, chopped	4 cups stock (pages 5–10) or water
1 tablespoon fennel seeds	1 teaspoon unrefined salt, or to taste
2 fennel bulbs, cored and chopped, fronds reserved for garnish	1 tablespoon fresh lemon juice, or to taste
	Freshly ground white or black pepper

Heat the oil in a large saucepan over medium-low heat. Add the shallots, cover, and cook until softened but not browned, about 5 minutes. Add the fennel seeds, cover, and cook for 3 minutes. Add the chopped fennel and garlic, cover, and cook for 10 minutes, or until softened. Add the stock and salt, increase the heat, and bring to a boil. Reduce the heat to low, cover, and simmer for 15 to 20 minutes, until the fennel is very soft.

Working in batches, transfer the soup to a blender and blend until mostly smooth. Return the soup to the pan, add the lemon juice, season generously with pepper, and add more salt if needed. Stir in half of the fennel fronds. Divide the soup among bowls, drizzle each with a little oil, and garnish with the remaining fennel fronds.

Cloud Soup

Here's a fanciful soup with delicate puffs of egg floating on the surface of a flavorful soup. Whimsical, yes! But easy and utterly pleasing. Indeed, fine cooking doesn't have to be fussy or complicated. While we find it perfect to share with girlfriends coming over for lunch, its texture and flavor is suitable for any age or gender. Or serve it when an otherwise substantial meal invites a light starter.

For people who think they can't eat borscht without something white on top, oblige them: Omit the yolk and serve their soup with a white cloud instead of the expected sour cream!

SERVES 4 AS A STARTER

5	cups stock (pages 5–10)	1	teaspoon chopped fresh chives
1¼	teaspoons unrefined salt	¼	teaspoon fresh lemon juice
1	large egg, separated		

In a large, wide sauté pan, bring the stock and 1 teaspoon of the salt to a simmer over medium heat.

Meanwhile, combine the egg yolk and chives in a small bowl. In a separate bowl, combine the egg white, the remaining ¼ teaspoon salt, and the lemon juice and beat with an electric beater until stiff but not dry. Fold the egg whites into the egg yolk mixture.

Gently drop the egg mixture, a teaspoon at a time, onto the surface of the simmering stock. Cover and cook over low heat for 1 to 2 minutes, just until the egg sets.

Ladle the stock into bowls, dividing the "clouds" evenly among the bowls.

Swanky Clouds

Make confetti-colored clouds by adding a tablespoon of edible flower blossoms; use only organic blossoms and remove and discard the calyx, stems, and other plant parts. Julienne large blossoms, such as rose petals, nasturtiums, pansies, or squash blossoms. Use small blossoms, such as violets, whole. Separate lilac blossoms or dandelion rays. Mince sprigs of blossoming herbs, such as thyme or oregano.

Nettle Soup with Poached Eggs

Back in the eleventh century, Milarepa, Tibet's most famous yogi and poet, lived for years by eating only stinging nettles. Enjoy a mess of them and this story is believable, for this fine-haired (when raw) veggie, with its 10 percent protein and remarkably high mineral content, contains and imparts more *qi* than does any other garden green. Cooking removes the nettles' sting (refrigeration retards it), and the leaves become velvety smooth but remain highly textured and full-bodied unlike any other vegetable we've tasted. As for flavor, think spinach without the oxalic acid edge and richer, sweeter, and heartier. Unlike brassicas, such as kale, collards, and bok choy, and daisy family greens, such as chicory, endive, and some lettuces, nettles aren't bitter.

With a good stock and a poached egg, this soup is a great restorative tonic. Nettles have anti-inflammatory properties and so are medicinal for rheumatism and gout; they also help stabilize blood sugar and soothe the kidney system, gastrointestinal tract, and nervous system. If nettles aren't available, substitute another tender potherb, such as spinach, mâche, lamb's quarters, or watercress. Serve this soup immediately, for if cooked and reheated, the nettles will color the stock.

SERVES 2

8	ounces fresh nettles
3	cups stock (pages 5–10)
½	teaspoon unrefined salt
2	large fresh eggs
	Freshly ground black pepper
1	teaspoon chopped fresh chives or scallions

Fresh Eggs Are Best for Poaching

While whole eggs store well refrigerated for up to six weeks, for the best poaching results, favor fresh eggs. As egg cartons sold in the United States are stamped with the Julian date (a number between 000 and 365) that they were packed, you can ascertain their freshness. A carton stamped with 000 means the eggs were packed on January 1 and a number of 90 means they were packed on April 1. You want a number only a few days to a week from the Julian date of the day you are purchasing the eggs. You'll also see an expiration date stamped to the right of the Julian date, which can be up to six weeks after the eggs were packed. For example, an egg carton stamped with the numbers 010 Feb 23 means that the eggs were packed on January 10 but the eggs can be sold until February 23.

If you have your own chickens, day-old eggs (rather than warm from the chicken) are better for poaching than just-laid eggs.

Where to Find Nettles

Look for nettles in your growers' market, forage them, or, better yet, if there's an undertrafficked, damp place in your garden, plant them. Rebecca has a nettle stand on the back side of the koi pond, and with a mild winter harvests them twelve months of the year. Raw nettles do sting, and so handling them with rubber gloves is advised. However, the sting, which contains histamine, serotonin, and formic acid, brings on, for most people, a minor tingling sensation that increases localized blood flow and thus can ease arthritic pain. Many people handle nettles without gloves.

Harvest only young stalks, for once nettles flower, their leaves develop gritty calcium carbonate deposits that may irritate the kidney system. Throughout the growing season the roots will continuously send up new shoots, so look below the flowering heads for less mature stalks waiting to be plucked.

Wearing rubber gloves, strip the nettles from the stems and coarsely chop the leaves. Set aside.

Pour the stock into a medium saucepan and add the salt. Place over medium heat and bring to a low simmer. Crack an egg into a fine-mesh strainer with a rounded bottom and gently swirl the egg over the sink to drain off a spoonful of the watery, loose part of the white. Place the remaining egg, still in the strainer, in the barely simmering stock and gently rotate the strainer for 10 seconds, or until the egg coalesces. Slide the egg out of the strainer and into the stock, and immediately repeat the straining process with the remaining egg. Immediately add the nettles, return the heat to a simmer, and simmer, uncovered, for 3 to 4 minutes, gently so as not to break the eggs, stirring the soup several times while the eggs and greens are cooking, until the whites are almost firm, the yolks still jiggles, and the nettles are tender.

Season with pepper, taste the soup, and adjust seasonings if needed. Ladle into the bowls with an egg in each, garnish with chives, and serve.

Chickpea Miso Broth with Okra and Enoki Mushrooms

As many gluten- and dairy-free people also do better without soy, here's fantastic news: There's a creamy sweet and wonderful miso that is soy-free. Chickpea miso boasts all the complex flavors of naturally fermented foods, plus it aids in digestion and assimilation. Miso soup is satisfying and sustaining; no wonder its regular consumption is linked with a reduction in breast cancer.

A cup of this broth makes a great start for any meal in any season. It's mostly about the creamy, rich stock, with the delicate veggie bits adding their own beauty and essence. Okra's flavor is reminiscent of both asparagus and eggplant, and its viscous, silky texture enhances any soup (it also helps soothe and heal an irritated digestive system).

To streamline preparation, use a strainer to "puree" the miso directly into the soup. (Alternatively, you may place the miso in a small dish, ladle broth from the soup into the miso, whisk them together, and stir into the soup.) If enoki mushrooms are not available, substitute four thinly sliced shiitake mushrooms, but add them along with the okra and wakame at the beginning of cooking rather than at the end.

SERVES 4

5	cups Kombu-Shiitake Stock (page 9)
1	cup thinly sliced okra (about 15 2- to 4-inch okra pods, about 10 ounces)
1½	tablespoons instant wakame flakes
1 to 1½	tablespoons finely grated fresh ginger (see note)
⅓ to ½	cup chickpea miso
1	(3.5-ounce) package enoki mushrooms, root ends trimmed off
2	scallions, thinly sliced on the diagonal

Combine the stock, okra, and wakame flakes in a large saucepan. Place over medium-high heat and bring to a simmer. Reduce the heat and simmer for 3 to 4 minutes, until the okra is tender.

Suspend a small strainer with a rounded bottom over a saucer. Hold the grated ginger in the palm of your hand and squeeze it to express 1 tablespoon of juice; add the juice to the soup and discard the pulp (or add it to your stock-making ingredients). Place ⅓ cup of the miso in the strainer, set the strainer into the soup, and with a spoon press the miso through the strainer and into the soup. Taste and add more miso or ginger to taste, if desired. Add the mushrooms and simmer for just 1 minute (do not boil), then add the scallions. Spoon into bowls and serve.

Note: When finely grated, a fresh and plump knob of ginger seemingly yields the same volume of juice! As it ages, it naturally dehydrates and so gives off less juice; also with age its bright, citrusy flavor decreases and its pungency intensifies. Keep the age of your ginger in mind when you're seasoning your soup.

Tamari and Toasted Sesame–Brushed Pork Rib Soup

While southerners may have the barbecue down, here's a new twist that gives the same crispy, tender meat and puts the pork bones to work; cooked low and slow in ample liquid the ribs impart their meaty essence to yield a substantial soup stock. The soup is further flavored by a variety of Asian seasonings and tart-sour tomatillos, with the succulent ribs set on top of the finished dish ready for you to dig in to at their peak point of crispness.

SERVES 4 TO 6

2	quarts water
1	(2-pound) rack pastured pork baby back ribs, cut into 4 sections
5	tablespoons tamari, or to taste
1	(3- to 4-inch) piece kombu
2	tablespoons chopped fresh ginger
1	tablespoon plus 1 teaspoon toasted sesame oil, or to taste
1	bunch baby turnips with greens attached, turnips quartered, greens ripped into pieces
8	ounces small tomatillos, husked, rinsed well, and quartered
2	tablespoons fresh lime juice, or to taste
8	ounces cooked thin rice noodles
3	scallions, light and green parts, thinly sliced
	A few handfuls of bean sprouts (optional)
	Coarsely ground toasted sesame seeds (optional)
	Lime wedges, for serving

In a large saucepan, combine the water and ribs. Place over high heat and bring to a boil. Reduce the heat and simmer, uncovered, for about 5 minutes, skimming off foam that rises to the surface. Add 3 tablespoons of the tamari, the kombu, and ginger and return the heat to a simmer. Immediately reduce the heat to low, cover, and cook at a low simmer for about 2 hours, until the ribs are tender but not quite falling off the bone, skimming foam—and, if you wish, fat—that rises to the surface.

Preheat the broiler.

Using tongs, transfer the ribs to a broiler pan and let cool. If you like, you can cut the ribs between the bone or simply leave them whole. In a small bowl, combine the remaining 2 tablespoons of tamari with 1 tablespoon of the toasted sesame oil. Brush the ribs on both sides with the tamari mixture and broil about 8 inches from the heat source for about 5 minutes, turning once, until the meat is crisp and browned. Keep warm.

Meanwhile, return the soup to a simmer, add the turnips and tomatillos, cover, and cook for about 5 minutes, until the vegetables are tender. Add the remaining 1 teaspoon of toasted sesame oil and the lime juice and turn off the heat.

Divide the noodles and turnip greens among bowls and ladle the broth into each along with some turnips and tomatillos. Set the ribs into the soup, top with the scallions and some bean sprouts and sesame seeds, if using, and serve with lime wedges alongside.

CREAMY SOUPS

Smoky Split Yellow Pea Soup with Spinach and Lime

This hearty, stick-to-your-ribs soup is a perfect cold-weather breakfast choice. The concept of soup for breakfast is not as odd as it may seem, as many cultures start their day with soup. The Japanese favor soup with fish and rice for breakfast, and for the Chinese it's congee, a long-simmered, rice-based soup (see our recipe on page 92). It may take a little getting used to, but eventually when you wake up your taste buds will wake up, too. And then anything goes—be it your standard eggs, last night's leftover pot roast, or this protein-rich, smoky-tangy soup. Or go the traditional route and make it for dinner, then heat up the leftovers for breakfast.

SERVES 4

¼ cup extra-virgin olive oil

1 medium red onion, chopped

4 garlic cloves, chopped

1 teaspoon ground cumin

½ teaspoon cumin seeds

½ teaspoon ground turmeric

¼ teaspoon cayenne pepper

1 cup dried split yellow peas, soaked in water to cover by a couple of inches overnight and drained

4 cups water or stock (pages 5–10)

1 teaspoon unrefined salt

1 tablespoon fresh lime juice, or to taste

2 cups chopped fresh spinach

½ teaspoon smoked paprika

Optional toppings: Avocado slices, chopped red onion, crumbled cooked bacon

In a large saucepan, heat 2 tablespoons of the oil over medium heat. Add the onion and cook until softened, about 5 minutes. Add the garlic and cook until softened and the onion starts to brown, about 5 minutes. Add the ground cumin, cumin seeds, turmeric, and cayenne and cook, stirring, for 1 minute. Add the split peas, water, and salt and bring to a boil. Reduce the heat, cover, and simmer for 1 hour, or until the split peas are softened but not mushy. Add the lime juice, then stir in the spinach until wilted.

In a small bowl, combine the remaining 2 tablespoons of oil with the smoked paprika and stir well. Spoon the soup into bowls and top each with a swirl of the smoky oil. Finish with the toppings, if using.

Choosing Quality Salt

While quality salt may be pricey, not all pricey salt is quality!

Salt imparts a substantial value to foods by heightening, deepening, and uniting savory flavors. We add it at the beginning of a soup so as it cooks the heat can drive the salt into the food to meld flavors, tenderize, and aid digestion. Then a pinch of salt at the end finishes the soup with a tang of bright flavor. If, that is, you're using good salt.

Taste a few grains of unrefined salt and the aftertaste is smooth, round, pleasurable and a little sweet. Unrefined salt has the highest percentage of important trace minerals, which gives it its rounder flavor. How to know if a salt is unrefined? Shop for salt that contains only one ingredient: salt. Terms to look for include "solar evaporated," "hand-harvested," or "hand-processed." Maldon salt and several brands of Celtic salt are among the top choices (but read labels carefully, as some Celtic salt is processed and contains additives). Quality salt starts from three dollars a pound, and considering how long a pound will last you, it's a small investment.

The aftertaste of refined salt, on the other hand, is harsh, sharp, and acrid. This category of salt includes table salt, kosher salt, Real Salt, and the currently trendy Himalayan and Hawaiian pink salts. By taste alone, you can tell that these salts have been kiln dried. The color of colored salt comes from clay from the salt beds. Your recipes are better off without them. If you doubt us, taste a few grains of any such salt; you'll find them comparable in taste to a generic salt from the supermarket shelf and nasty in comparison to a quality unrefined salt.

Cultured White Gazpacho

For all you fans of fermentation out there, here's one to add to your cultured-foods repertoire—first we'll learn how to make sour cream from cashews, then we'll use the sour cream as the basis of this white gazpacho (traditional white gazpacho is made from almonds). Cashew Sour Cream (page 103) lends a creamy texture and delightful cultured tang that plays off the subtly sweet grapes and coolness of the cucumber. The soup is refreshing but substantial, so we often enjoy it in smallish bowlfuls or even little shot glass hits for a between-meal snack or aperitif.

SERVES 6

1	recipe Cashew Sour Cream (page 103)		1	tablespoon fresh lemon juice, or to taste
1	large seedless cucumber, peeled and chopped		½	teaspoon unrefined salt, or to taste
2	cups seedless green grapes		¼	teaspoon freshly ground white pepper
1	large shallot, chopped		¼	cup extra-virgin olive oil
1 to 2	garlic cloves, cut in half			Garnishes: Minced cucumber, minced fresh dill, sliced grapes

In a blender, combine all the ingredients except the oil and garnishes and blend until smooth. Slowly add the oil through the hole in the top and blend until homogenous. Pour into a container and refrigerate; serve cold, topped with your choice of garnishes.

Cream of Mushroom Soup

The cream of mushroom soup that Rebecca's mother made—featuring meadow mushrooms that the whole clan gathered—was without par. Grandma in her blue Buick and Grandpa in his green Buick would each load up a carful of cousins—in those pre-seatbelt days, a lot of little bodies could cram into one car—and a-foraging they'd go. In this adaptation of the family recipe, Rebecca favors coconut milk over the wheat-based roux and dairy cream, and even her mom finds it simply delicious.

Serve a bowl of it with a large salad for a light warm-weather supper or a cup of it to accompany a more substantial cold-weather meal.

SERVES 4

2	tablespoons extra-virgin olive or virgin coconut oil
1	onion, minced
1	pound finely chopped mixed mushrooms with stems (about 4 cups)
1	celery stalk, diced
1	teaspoon minced fresh thyme, or ¼ teaspoon dried
1	teaspoon unrefined salt
3	cups stock (pages 5–10)
1	cup coconut milk
¼	teaspoon Hungarian paprika
	Freshly grated nutmeg
	Freshly ground black or white pepper
¼	cup chopped fresh chives

Heat the oil in a large saucepan over medium heat. Add the onion, mushrooms, and celery and sauté for about 5 minutes, until the vegetables are softened. Add the thyme and cook for 1 minute more. Add the salt and stock and bring to a simmer. Cover and simmer for 15 minutes. Stir in the coconut milk and bring just to a simmer—watch carefully to prevent the coconut milk from boiling and separating. Remove from the heat, add the paprika, and season with nutmeg and pepper.

Leave the soup as is, partially blend it in a blender or by using an immersion blender, or blend completely in a regular blender. Divide the soup among bowls, garnish with the chives, and serve.

Choosing Quality Oils and Fats

It's hard to imagine a fat-free soup. That's because even a single spoonful of nutritious fat in your soup helps bring out the flavors of the other ingredients and imparts a sense of comfort and satiety. And because fat is denser than water or steam, a sautéed onion, for example, has greater flavor range and depth and conveys more warmth and energy than does a raw, boiled, or steamed onion.

Now let's talk about quality of the various types of oils and the heat they can withstand. Be forewarned: You'll find some of this information counter to popular conception.

Liquid Vegetable Oils (Polyunsaturated Fats)

A plant's fatty acids, found in its reproductive parts, store sunlight energy and contain more flavor and aroma than the rest of the plant. They're precious stuff. Befitting their preciousness, fatty acids require careful handling to protect their integrity. The essential fatty acids are the most fragile and are quickly destroyed by light, oxygen, and heat.

Unrefined (extra-virgin) oil tastes and smells just like the food from which it was made. Thus unrefined olive oil unmistakably smells and tastes like olives, and likewise hazelnut oil smells and tastes like hazelnuts. A spoonful is delicious, vital, and refreshing in your mouth, whereas refined oils feel greasy, viscous, and unpalatable in your mouth and are completely removed from their source in terms of smell and taste. Isn't it affirming that you can trust your own sensory perceptions to know which oils are best!

Unfortunately, the vast majority of vegetable oils are refined. Temperatures exceeding 500°F and caustic bleaches and deodorizers denature their delicate fatty acids and strip their flavor and aroma. Furthermore—and this is chilling—this triggers free radical formation and makes refined oils carcinogenic. Poor-quality fats suppress the immune system, challenge the liver and digestive system, and exacerbate cancer, candidiasis, tumors, cysts, edema, obesity, and some forms of high blood pressure.

While the designation for unrefined olive oil is "extra-virgin," unfortunately some unscrupulous producers dilute their aromatic and flavorful extra-virgin oil with cheap refined oil, olive or otherwise, which has no flavor or aroma. Purchase only extra-virgin olive oil from a reputable manufacturer; pass on refined olive oils, including "pure," "natural," and "pomace" olive oil.

So the quality of the oil is critical. Equally critical is that you do not heat oils above their optimum temperature range. Thus oils containing omega-3 fatty acids, such as canola, flax, and walnut oils, should never be heated. Oils high in omega-6 fatty acids, such as sesame, sunflower, and peanut oil, tolerate temperatures up to 260°F, and oils high in omega-9 fatty acids, such as olive, macadamia, and hazelnut oils may safely be heated to 325°F. Heat damages oil in two ways: first, it accelerates their rancidity, and second, and it distorts their molecules. It's crucial to only use liquid vegetable oils processed at low temperatures and to not heat them above their safe point. That's why the best fats for frying, searing, and baking are saturated fats (see below).

Before we go further, realize that the much touted "smoke point" and guidelines for "high heat" oils are bogus. An oil's smoke point is when it becomes so hot that it releases a bluish smoke and grows close to combusting. These smoke vapors turn into acrolein, a varnishlike substance that gums up your kitchen walls and lungs, irritates your throat and eyes, and, if the fat is consumed, is toxic to your liver. But it's important to know that fats are denatured long before they reach their smoke point. An oil's safe point is typically several hundred degrees lower than its smoke point. For example, canola oil's smoke point is 470°F, but its omega-3s are denatured when heated above 100°F. Do not use liquid vegetable oils for searing, deep frying, or cooking above their ideal temperature range.

Saturated Vegetable Oils (Monounsaturated Fats)

Unrefined (extra-virgin) coconut oil and red palm oil are semisolid fats that withstand temperatures above 325°F and therefore are excellent for searing, frying, and baking. As with liquid vegetable oils, unrefined coconut oil tastes and smells like coconut, and therefore it's limited to dishes wanting a coconut flavor. While red palm oil imbues food with a lovely orange color, its flavor is, for many people, an acquired taste. Note that when red palm oil is initially heated, some of its tiny palm particles have an initial "burn-off"; this is not to be confused with its smoke point.

Saturated Animal Fats

Happily, lard and chicken fat (schmaltz) do not taste like pork or chicken, but they do impart umami flavor and can be safely heated to temperatures above 325°F.

Favoring quality oils requires vigilance. Most oils, even many found in natural food stores, are made of refined oil, including many vegetable oils and every olive oil that's not labeled "extra-virgin." You can discern by using the guidelines above or smelling and tasting the oils. Don't use anything but quality oils in your cooking.

Carrot Soup with Garlic Chips

arrot soup is an everyday classic; now you can have it any day, dairy free. A small amount of rice blended with the soup provides the thickness and creaminess we're after in a cream-based soup (something you can do with just about any soup that needs thickening), and garlic chips add an element of crunch. Anytime of year is a good time for this soup, but we especially enjoy it in the fall, as its rich gold-orange harvest color so perfectly fits the season.

SERVES 4 TO 6

SOUP

2	tablespoons extra-virgin olive oil
1	medium onion, chopped
2	garlic cloves, chopped
2	tablespoons uncooked white rice
1	teaspoon ground cumin
½	teaspoon ground turmeric
¼	teaspoon paprika
⅛ to ¼	teaspoon cayenne pepper, to taste
1	pound carrots, sliced
6	cups stock (pages 5–10) or water
1½	teaspoons unrefined salt
1	tablespoon fresh lime juice, or to taste
2	tablespoons minced fresh parsley (optional)

GARLIC CHIPS

¼	cup extra-virgin olive oil
4	garlic cloves, thinly sliced

Make the soup: Heat the oil in a large saucepan over medium heat. Add the onion and sauté until very soft, about 10 minutes. Add the garlic and cook for another minute. Add the rice and cook for 5 minutes. Add the cumin, turmeric, paprika, and cayenne and cook for 2 minutes.

Add the carrots, stock, and salt. Increase the heat to high and bring to a boil, then reduce the heat to low, cover, and simmer for 30 minutes.

Meanwhile, make the garlic chips: Heat the oil with the garlic slices in a single layer in a tiny pot (a sturdy 1-cup stainless-steel measuring cup is a good choice) or small skillet over medium heat for 3 to 5 minutes, until the garlic is golden and slightly crisp. Remove the garlic from the oil using a slotted spoon and drain it on a plate lined with paper towels. Reserve the oil for finishing the soup.

Transfer the soup to a blender and blend until smooth. Return the soup to the saucepan, adjust the seasonings, and stir in the lime juice.

Spoon into bowls and serve, sprinkled with parsley, if using, and topped with the garlic chips and a swirl of the garlic-flavored oil.

Choosing Quality Ingredients

Many a time we've shared a food as simple as a bowl of chicken soup and we're asked for the recipe. While there's really not that much difference between basic chicken soup recipes, ingredient quality ranges from marginal to excellent, and therein lies the difference between a food that merely fills and one that is memorable.

You can easily discern this for yourself. Make two batches of any dish using generic ingredients in one and in the other, use *only* quality ingredients (down to and including the salt). Now do a taste test, blindfolded or otherwise, and you'll readily taste and "feel" the difference between superior and shoddy.

Happily, the best-tasting chicken soup is also best for your health. Quality ingredients, incidentally, don't necessarily mean the most expensive, but knowing which ingredients are best requires being informed.

Organic: Buying organic is voting with your fork. Favor organic foods whenever possible, for their extra flavor and greater nutritional value and for the superior energy they impart. Chemically grown foods take their

toll on your kidneys and liver (the organs that filter chemicals) as well as on the environment. We're barely four generations into ingesting artificial chemicals, and judging from the results, it's been a disastrous experiment. While organic is one quality determination, it's not necessarily enough; a carrot or chicken produced by an organic megafarm substantively differs from one produced by a small farmer who is in the business to provide quality food for both his or her own family and the larger community.

Seasonal and Regional Produce: In the summer, a local zucchini or watermelon is winsome. In January, little positive can be said for either of these long-distance travelers other than that the melon is wet. An easy way to favor seasonal and regional food is to garden and/or purchase from your local growers' market and from the stores that support local farmers.

Unrefined, Whole, Unprocessed Foods: Favoring whole, intact foods builds your health. Refined foods have had something taken away from them and, therefore, are not as *whole*some. Minimally refined foods that you can duplicate in your own home kitchen are in a different league than are today's highly processed foods. For example, at home you can extract extra-virgin coconut oil from a coconut or olive oil from olives, but you cannot produce "lite" olive oil or an aroma-free coconut oil. Highly processed foods resemble nothing you could grow in your garden or produce in your home. They've been stripped, colored, extruded, refined, bleached, injected, hydrogenated, genetically modified, irradiated, gassed, and grown with hormones, fertilizers, pesticides, antifungal agents, and herbicides.

No matter what the FDA claims or what slick marketing strategies exhort, ignore newfangled ingredients and products. Rely on whole foods that for thousands of years have promoted human health.

Minty Avocado and Tomatillo Soup

As the coauthor of two raw foods cookbooks, Leda is well versed in the world of uncooked vegetable-based soups. Here she melds that information with a traditional foods approach by basing the soup on bone stock to elevate both the flavor and healing potential of the soup, and in doing so harvesting the best from both the raw and the cooked schools. See page 2 for the health benefits of developing a stock-making habit; enjoying cooling summer soups such as this one is a great way of extending your stock habit into the hottest days of the year. Serve this one as part of a light meal, a midday snack, or even sipped with a straw as a savory smoothie alternative.

SERVES 2 TO 4

2	cups Bone Stock (page 5), Vegetable Stock (page 8), or water
1	small avocado, peeled, pitted, and flesh scooped out
4	large tomatillos, peeled, rinsed well, and quartered

1	medium cucumber, peeled and chopped
	Large handful of fresh mint leaves
3	tablespoons fresh lemon juice, or to taste
1½	teaspoons unrefined salt, or to taste

Combine all the ingredients in a blender and blend on high speed until smooth, adding more stock or water if the soup is too thick. Taste and adjust the seasonings with salt and/or lemon juice, if needed. Serve straight from the blender, or cover and refrigerate and serve chilled.

VARIATION:

Smoky-Minty Avocado and Tomatillo Soup: Add ⅛ to ¼ teaspoon of chipotle powder (or smoked paprika, for milder tastes).

Leek and Scallion Soup with Garlic Cream

Gently poaching generous amounts of garlic in olive oil results in creamy, sweet cloves that are mellowed of their pungent bite. That's how we're able to add a whole head of garlic in here, and in so doing turn a vegetable soup into a cream of vegetable soup. Two more allium family members make it into the mix: subtly onion-flavored leeks for the soup base and scallions in the raw for a more pronounced-flavored finish. The garlic cream itself can be used as a thickener in other soup recipes.

If you don't have stock in the house, try making an impromptu leek stock to use in your soup: Rinse the dark green leek leaves, chop them roughly, place in a large saucepan, and add water to cover. Throw in any other vegetables you might have—a carrot, onion, or a couple of garlic cloves, for example—then bring to a boil, reduce the heat to very low, cover, and cook at a bare simmer for 45 minutes. Strain through a fine-mesh strainer into a heatproof bowl and use as you would any other stock. Or save your leek greens to add to a later batch of Bone Stock (page 5) or Vegetable Stock (page 8).

SERVES 4

SOUP

2	tablespoons extra-virgin olive oil
4	large leeks, white and light green parts only, rinsed well and chopped
1	celery stalk, chopped
1	teaspoon dried thyme
2	tablespoons white wine
1	large potato, peeled and chopped
4	cups stock (pages 5–10) or water
	Unrefined salt and freshly ground white or black pepper

GARLIC CREAM

Cloves from 1 medium garlic head, peeled (do not smash)

2	tablespoons extra-virgin olive oil
1	cup water
1½	tablespoons fresh lemon juice, or to taste
2	scallions, white and green parts, thinly sliced

Make the soup: Heat the oil in a large saucepan over medium heat. Add the leeks and celery and cook until softened, about 5 minutes. Stir in the thyme. Add the wine and cook until evaporated. Add the potato and stock, season with salt and pepper, and bring to a simmer. Reduce the heat and simmer for about 15 minutes, until the potato is softened.

Meanwhile, make the garlic cream: In a small saucepan, combine the garlic, oil, and water. Bring to a simmer over medium heat, then reduce the heat, partially cover, and simmer for about 20 minutes, until the garlic is softened throughout. Add the garlic and liquid to the soup.

Working in two batches, pour the soup into a blender and blend until smooth. Return to the pan and heat through. Add the lemon juice, taste, and adjust the seasonings with salt, pepper, and/or lemon juice as needed. Spoon into bowls and serve, topped with the scallions and a drizzle of oil.

Cream of Fava Soup with Cumin, Mint, and Salt-Preserved Lemon

This soup is an inspiration from Peggy Markel, Rebecca's friend who has operated culinary tours based in Florence, Italy, and Marrakech, Morocco, for more than twenty years. Peggy artfully uses favorite Moroccan flavors cumin, mint, and preserved lemon to complement and brighten the earthy fava beans, resulting in this velvety soup with a zing.

Look for fresh fava beans in vibrantly green pods, for as the beans mature the pods develop black splotches and the skin of the beans develops a slightly bitter taste. Peggy reports that while the French remove fava skins regardless of their maturity, the Italians are less inclined to peel them, and the Moroccans not only don't peel the beans but they cook the entire young pods. What will be your pleasure? Taste the peel to determine whether you'd like the skins in the soup or not. Peggy's rule of thumb is to remove the skins once the beans become as large as a lima bean.

If the thought of shelling and, perhaps, peeling all those beans seems intimidating, do as Peggy does: "Shell them with a friend or take advantage of the contemplative pause if affords to sit and shell, listen to music, and gaze out the window. It goes quickly if you give into it."

This soup is delicious either hot or chilled.

SERVES 4

3	pounds unshelled fava beans (2 cups shelled and peeled beans)
¼	cup extra-virgin olive oil, plus more for drizzling
2	shallots, thinly sliced
1	small fennel bulb, cored and thinly sliced
½	teaspoon ground cumin
½	teaspoon unrefined salt
	Juice from ½ lemon
¼	salt-preserved lemon (see page 56), cut into julienne, or 1 fresh lemon, quartered
	Whole or minced fresh mint leaves

Shell the fava beans and skin or peel the beans if you like (see headnote). If the beans are young and vibrantly fresh, they'll be easy to peel: Simply tear an opening in one end, and then using your thumb and forefinger, squirt out the bean. To peel more mature beans, parboil them for 1 minute, strain, and cool. Then, as above, tear an opening in one end, and using your thumb and forefinger, squirt out the bean. Set the beans aside.

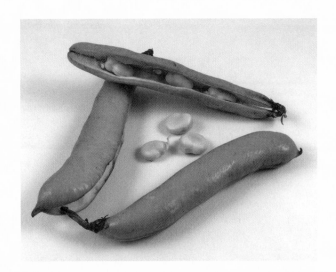

Heat the oil in a medium saucepan over medium heat. Add the shallots and fennel and sweat for about 5 minutes, until they become transparent but not browned. Add the fava beans and cook for about 5 minutes, until they turn a vibrant green color. Add the cumin and salt. Add water to cover the fava beans, bring to a simmer, then reduce the heat and simmer for 15 to 20 minutes, until the fava beans soften and start to crack open. Add more water, if necessary, to keep the vegetables covered.

Blend until creamy, using an immersion blender or in a regular blender. If the puree is too thick, add a bit of warm water. Add the lemon juice and season with additional salt if needed. Divide the soup into bowls, garnish with the salt-preserved lemon and mint, drizzle with oil, and serve.

Salt-Preserved Lemons

Preserved lemons can be found in Middle Eastern grocery stores, but making your own is easy; all that's required is patience as the salt works its magic for the thirty days it takes to "pickle" the lemons. The flavor indeed is salty (some people like to give theirs a light rinse before using) and deeply lemony but mellowed of the tartness found in a fresh lemon. A small amount is all that's needed to accent a soup, stew, or other dish.

MAKES 5 TO 8 PRESERVED LEMONS

¼	cup fine unrefined salt
5 or 6	organic unwaxed lemons, scrubbed well and dried
	Fresh lemon juice, if needed

Sprinkle 1 tablespoon of the salt in the bottom of a quart-size glass jar with a tight-fitting lid. Trim off the rounded part at the stem end of five lemons and quarter the lemons from the top to within ½ inch of the bottom (without cutting all the way through) to make an X-shaped incision into the lemons. Pack the remaining 3 tablespoons of salt into the exposed flesh, then reshape the fruit. Pack the lemons into the jar vertically side by side and push them down to release their juices and to make room for all the lemons. Add a sixth lemon, prepared the same way, if it can fit. Leave at least 1 inch of space remaining at the top and put the lid on the jar. The next day, press down on the lemons again so they can release more juice as they soften. Do this again for another day or two, until the lemons are completely covered in liquid; if necessary, supplement with fresh lemon juice, making sure there is always at least 1 inch of space at the top. Tightly cover and place the lemons in a cool spot out of direct sunlight for 30 days, turning the jar upside down once a day to evenly distribute the juices. Transfer to the refrigerator; they will keep refrigerated for about a year.

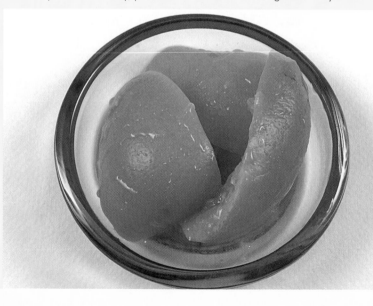

Radish-Top Soup with Salted Radishes

Don't let your radish tops wilt away in the crisper drawer; take advantage of them while they're fresh, as these peppery greens are completely edible, nutritious (they're filled with vitamin C), and the base for a most sophisticated soup. Separate the greens from the roots after purchasing, and wash and store them loosely wrapped in the refrigerator for no more than one or two days, as they are fragile. Young spring radishes generally have the mildest of leaves.

Try any type of radish with its leaves for this soup, from the most common Cherry Belle to the carrot-shaped icicle and the magenta-fleshed watermelon radish. It's worth seeking out farmers' market fresh radishes for the most vibrant, crispest, and tastiest greens. Older greens are more peppery, so taste first and, if necessary, mellow their bite by swapping in some spinach, chard, or another milder green in the soup. Radish greens can also be added to pesto, salads, or stir-fries.

SERVES 4 TO 6

3 tablespoons extra-virgin olive oil, lard, or virgin coconut oil

2 large bunches radishes with vibrant-looking leaves (about 6 cups lightly packed)

1½ pounds red- or yellow-skinned potatoes, peeled and cut into 1-inch pieces

5 cups stock (pages 5–10)

Salt and freshly ground black pepper

⅓ cup Cashew Sour Cream (page 103)

Separate the leaves from the radishes at the point where the stem joins the radishes; wash and dry them. Thinly slice or julienne the radishes, place them in a bowl, and lightly rub a little salt into them to wilt them. Set the radishes aside.

Heat the oil in a large saucepan over medium heat. Add the radish leaves and cook, stirring a couple of times, until wilted, about 2 minutes. Add the potatoes and stock, bring to a simmer, then cover, reduce the heat to low, and simmer until the potatoes are tender, about 15 minutes. Season with salt and pepper and stir in the sour cream.

Transfer the soup to a blender in batches and blend until smooth. Return the soup to the pan and gently reheat until just hot if necessary. Taste and adjust the seasonings if needed, then spoon into bowls. Drain the radishes, add to the soup bowls as a garnish, and serve.

Mulligatawny Soup

The typical mulligatawny soup you'll find on an Indian restaurant menu is a lentil-based vegetarian one; the lentil version has become so standard that Leda's husband, Nash, who is as Anglo-Indian as is this soup, was surprised when he was served this chicken-based mulligatawny thickened with chickpea flour. But mulligatawny variations abound, and this one is every bit as authentic, combining British and Indian ingredients for a spicy, slightly sweet, and substantial dish, more a curry than a soup and a complete meal in a bowl. To further thicken your soup, try adding some coconut milk during the last minute or two of cooking, just long enough to heat it through.

SERVES 4 TO 6

1	tablespoon extra-virgin olive oil, plus more if needed
1	pound organic boneless dark chicken, cut into 1-inch pieces
1	large onion, chopped
1	Granny Smith apple, peeled, cored, and cut into ½-inch cubes
1½	tablespoons minced fresh ginger
3	garlic cloves, minced
1½	teaspoons mild or hot curry powder
1	teaspoon ground cumin
1	teaspoon ground coriander
¼	teaspoon ground turmeric
¼ to ½	teaspoon ground cayenne (optional)
6	cups stock (pages 5–10)
2	tablespoons chickpea flour

Unrefined salt	1½	cups cooked rice or other grain
1 tablespoon fresh lemon juice, or to taste		Handful of fresh cilantro leaves, chopped

Heat the oil in a large saucepan over medium-high heat. Add the chicken and cook until lightly browned, stirring a few times, about 5 minutes, refraining from stirring for the first couple of minutes so the chicken gets a nice sear and doesn't stick to the bottom of the pan. Using a slotted spoon, transfer the chicken to a bowl.

Add the onion and apple to the fat in the pan, adding more oil if the pan is dry, and cook, stirring often, until the onion is well browned, 7 to 10 minutes. Add the ginger and garlic and cook, stirring, for 2 minutes. Add the curry powder, cumin, coriander, turmeric, and cayenne, if using, and cook, stirring, for 30 seconds. Return the chicken to the pan.

Add 5 cups of the stock and bring to a simmer; meanwhile, whisk the chickpea flour into the remaining 1 cup of stock (if lumps form that can't be whisked out, blend it, using an immersion blender or a regular blender) and add it to the pot. Season with salt, reduce the heat to low, cover, and simmer for 30 minutes. Add the lemon juice, taste, and adjust the flavors with salt and/or lemon juice if needed. Stir in the rice and cilantro, spoon into bowls, and serve.

Curry, Curry Powder, and Curry Leaves

Curry is a highly seasoned dish that spans nations, from India to Sri Lanka and Pakistan and Japan. About 23 million people regularly eat curry worldwide, and curry has become a national dish of the United Kingdom.

Curry is perhaps most associated with Indian cuisine, but curry powder is not. Curry powder is a golden yellow spice blend typically based on turmeric, coriander, cumin, and other ingredients, and its roots are more Western than Indian, most likely dating back to the eighteenth century as British and Indian cuisine bumped into each other, which is why a soup such as mulligatawny can contain curry powder and still be authentically Indian.

Curry leaves, on the other hand, bear no relation to curry powder; they come from the curry tree, and their flavor is slightly bitter, pungent, and citruslike. They're a core component in South Indian cooking; we use them in our Pepper Water with Beef (page 16), and they're an indispensable ingredient in the menu of Dosa Kitchen, Leda and Nash's Brattleboro, Vermont–based food truck featuring specialties of that region's cuisine.

Puree of Asparagus with Dill

The delicate sweetness of a stem of meadow grass hints at the incomparable flavor of fresh local asparagus. To heighten this flavor, we'll flash-cook thinly sliced asparagus in a rich soup stock. Here a rich stock is imperative, as water or even a stock made of asparagus ends would be too thin to carry the essence. Besides, we'll get more mileage from the stem ends by peeling them and using them in the soup. It's best to bypass wimpy off-season asparagus for this recipe.

Fresh dill makes a nice finish to this soup, as would a small amount of minced salt-preserved lemon (see page 56). The soup is delicious served cold when the weather is hot.

SERVES 4

2	tablespoons extra-virgin olive oil, plus more for drizzling
2	shallots, chopped
1	teaspoon ground cumin
1	medium yellow potato, peeled and chopped
5 to 6	cups stock (pages 5–10)
1½	teaspoons unrefined salt, or to taste
2	bunches asparagus (about 2½ pounds)
1	tablespoon fresh lemon juice, or to taste
½	teaspoon freshly ground white pepper, or to taste
2	tablespoons chopped fresh dill

Heat the oil in a large saucepan over medium heat. Add the shallots and sauté for about 3 minutes, until translucent. Add the cumin and cook for 1 minute more. Add the potato, 5 cups of the stock, and the salt, increase the heat, and bring to a boil. Cover the pan, reduce the heat, and simmer for about 12 minutes, until the potato is softened.

While the potato is cooking, snap off the bottom few inches of the asparagus stalks and peel and discard the fibrous skin from the ends. Thinly slice all parts of the stalks. Add the asparagus slices to the soup, bring the heat back to a simmer, and simmer for 1 to 2 minutes, until the asparagus is just tender. Use an immersion blender or regular blender to puree the soup, adding more stock if the soup is too thick. Return the soup to the pot and reheat, if necessary. Add the lemon juice and pepper, taste, and adjust the seasonings as needed. Divide the soup into bowls, add a drizzle of oil and the dill, and serve.

Cream of Tomato and Beet Soup

This deep crimson–hued soup is the answer to borscht when time is short. Coconut milk rather than the standard sour cream provides its creaminess; for the full alternative-borscht effect, top with our take on sour cream made from cultured cashews.

If you don't have stock already made or you're falling short of a quart, supplement with the beets' cooking water, or use the cooking water as the base for your next batch of stock. And don't toss the beet greens, as they are extremely edible. We love them for their earthy, slightly mineral taste and how healthful they are: they're packed with fiber, contain more iron than spinach, and their nutritional value rivals that of the beets themselves.

SERVES 4 TO 6

1	pound medium beets, scrubbed well, greens finely chopped, if available
2	tablespoons extra-virgin olive oil
1	large red onion, chopped
1½	teaspoons ground caraway, plus more for garnish
1	(15-ounce) can diced tomatoes with juices
1	quart stock (pages 5–10)
	Unrefined salt and freshly ground black pepper
1	cup coconut milk
2	tablespoons fresh lime juice, or to taste
	Cashew Sour Cream (page 103; optional)
2	tablespoons finely chopped fresh dill

Place the beets in a large saucepan and add water to cover. Place over medium-high heat and bring to a boil; reduce the heat to medium and simmer for about 1 hour, adding more water if needed to keep the beets submerged, until tender (test one by inserting a paring knife into a beet; when it encounters no resistance, it's done). Using a slotted spoon, remove the beets from the water (reserve the water if you like; see headnote) and let cool slightly, then peel and chop them.

Rinse out and dry the saucepan, then heat the oil over medium heat. Add the onion and cook until softened, about 5 minutes. Add the caraway and cook for 1 minute. Add the tomatoes, chopped beets, and stock. Season with salt and pepper, increase the heat, and bring to a boil. Reduce the heat to low, cover, and simmer for 20 minutes to blend the flavors.

Working in batches, puree the soup in a blender. Return to the pan, add the coconut milk, and heat until heated through. Add the lime juice, taste, and adjust the seasonings with lime juice, salt, and/or pepper if needed. Ladle into bowls, top each with a dollop of sour cream, if using, the reserved beet greens, if using, the dill, and a little caraway, and serve.

STEWS AND EXTRA-HEARTY SOUPS

Buffalo Chili

A friend of ours fondly recalls her family's celebratory bowl of chili every single Friday night of the year. This recipe is up for such devotion, for when the gestalt of buffalo melds with a Tex-Mex-style chili, you'll want it again and again. What's buffalo gestalt? Using your "felt sense," imagine the energy of a buffalo. Now do the same for the following: a carrot, peach, clam, and chicken. Next, pay attention to how you "feel" after eating each food. Indeed, each food imparts its own type of energy. We always enjoy an extra sense of oomph after eating buffalo. (If buffalo is unavailable, beef makes a fine substitute; to adjust the recipe for beef, brown the beef over medium-high heat and increase the cooking time of the chili from 5 minutes to 20 minutes.)

For the deepest and most authentic flavor, we use roasted chiles. How hot you like it will determine which chiles you use. To play it safe, use a mild chile, such as an Anaheim or Hatch, or a broad-shouldered chile, such as a poblano. To go for broke, add a few jalapeños or habaneros.

You may easily double or quadruple this recipe. Also, according to your taste, feel free to increase the beans and decrease the meat, or vice versa. The recipe is great as is, and it also welcomes your tweaking it according to what you have on hand. If you're from the "need-a-dollop-of-sour-cream-on-the-chili" school, then yes, this chili may look a little naked in your bowl. So, play with your expectations. For example, go more authentic. Consider that chili was around long before dairy-producing animals were introduced in the 1500s, and so sour cream is an upstart. Instead, serve your chili with Amaranth Crisps (page 104), made from the Aztecs' sacred grain. Or go for the sour cream; just make it our dairy-free Cashew Sour Cream (page 103).

SERVES 6

3 tablespoons extra-virgin olive oil, unrefined sesame oil, or red palm oil

2 teaspoons cumin seeds

4 garlic cloves, minced

1 large onion, finely chopped

2 poblano, Anaheim, or other chiles, roasted (see sidebar) and chopped

4 cups cooked pinto or anasazi beans, drained (see page 73)

2 cups stock (pages 5–10) or water, plus more if needed

2 ripe small to medium tomatoes, chopped, or 1 (15-ounce) can chopped tomatoes

1 pound ground pastured buffalo or beef

Unrefined salt

½ cup chopped fresh cilantro

1 tablespoon fresh lime juice, or to taste

Heat 2 tablespoons of the oil in a large saucepan over medium heat. Add the cumin and cook for about 1 minute, until it is one shade darker and aromatic. Add the garlic and onion and sauté for about 5 minutes, until the onion is softened. Add the roasted chiles, beans, and stock. Add the tomatoes, bring the heat to a simmer, and simmer for 15 minutes.

Meanwhile, heat the remaining 1 tablespoon oil a large skillet over medium-low heat. Add the buffalo and, using a spatula, flatten it out to cover the pan's surface. Cook until it just starts to brown (see sidebar), about 4 minutes, then turn and lightly brown the other side, about 2 minutes. Remove from the heat and, using the spatula, coarsely break the buffalo into chunks.

Add the meat and its drippings to the bean mixture and season with salt. Simmer for 5 minutes to blend the flavors. Adjust the seasonings, stir in the cilantro and lime juice, and serve.

Buffalo (aka Bison) Cooks Faster Than Beef

Buffalo tastes sweeter, is darker in color, lower in calories, leaner, and higher in protein than beef and is best when cooked over medium-low heat for a short time. For this dish, cook the buffalo just until the edges start to brown and add it to the chili for just the last 5 minutes of cooking.

How to Roast Chiles

Although chiles originated in the Americas, they're a popular seasoning agent throughout the world. Chile-using cuisines outside of the Americas are yet to catch on to our native roasting secret; we often use roasted chiles in Asian, African, and Middle Eastern dishes for the smoky sweetness they impart and invite you to try the same.

Place chiles directly over hot coals or a gas burner or under an electric broiler. Roast, turning frequently, for about 10 minutes, until the skin is blistered and blackened all over. Place in a paper or plastic bag, seal, and allow to steam for 10 to 15 minutes, until the skin has loosened and the chiles are cool enough to handle. Put on rubber or disposable gloves and push and/or rub off the charred skin under running water. Pull out the cores, cut in half, and remove the membranes and seeds. Hold under running water to rinse off any remaining blackened skin or seeds. Slice in half lengthwise and remove and discard the seeds.

Yucatán Turkey Thigh and Yucca Soup

Preconquest ingredients were gluten and dairy free, turkey was the bird in the pot, and the tuber yucca was a staple starchy ingredient in Central America. That makes upstarts of the onion, garlic, chicken, pasta, dairy, carrots, celery, and olive oil that appear in many contemporary Yucatán chicken soups. If you can't imagine this soup without garlic or onions, scratch history and include them—but our version is the real deal and quite wonderful.

While yucca is mild flavored, its silky, smooth starch adds an ambience to other soup ingredients that rivals that of the mighty potato. When purchasing fresh yucca, pick tubers that are firm, well formed, and blemish-free with a clean, fresh scent. Store whole yucca in a cool, dark, dry place for up to a week. Or peel, cover with water, and refrigerate for up to five days. As yucca is relatively hard to peel and chop, it is convenient to purchase this tuber peeled, cut into wedges, and frozen; frozen yucca is available in many supermarkets.

This soup is perfect for those times when there's no stock on hand but you're looking for the inimitable heft a good bone stock gives a dish. If your market doesn't offer turkey thighs, use chicken. Although Mexican oregano is similarly flavored to Mediterranean oregano, they're unrelated, with the Mexican variety featuring both citrus and licorice notes.

Turkey thigh soup is decidedly home style, with bits of cartilage inevitably ending up in the soup. If company is coming, you may bypass the potential gristle issue by substituting turkey breast for the thigh and using bone stock instead of water. While this soup is great au blanc, you may first brown the thigh. For yet another pre-Columbian note, serve with either Amaranth Crisps (page 104) or Griddle-Cooked Masa Harina and Daikon Flatbread (page 110).

SERVES 4

1 bone-in, skin-on pastured turkey thigh, or 4 bone-in, skin-on pastured chicken thighs	2 serrano chiles, roasted (see page 67) and chopped
2 cups peeled and chopped yucca	1½ teaspoons unrefined salt, or to taste
2 tomatoes (about 1 pound), peeled, cored, seeded, and chopped	4 teaspoons chopped fresh oregano, preferably Mexican (see sidebar), or 1½ teaspoons dried
1 poblano chile, roasted (see page 67) and chopped	¼ cup fresh lime juice
	1 avocado, peeled, pitted, and roughly chopped

Place the turkey thigh in a large saucepan. Add water to cover, cover the pot, and place over medium-high heat. Bring to a boil, then reduce the heat and simmer for 5 minutes, skimming off and discarding any foam that forms at the top.

Meanwhile, peel the yucca, cut it into 2-inch lengths, then cut the lengths in half vertically. Remove the small central fibrous core, slice the pieces lengthwise, and chop. Add the yucca, tomatoes, chiles, and salt to the pan. Return the heat to a simmer, then cover and simmer for about 2 hours, until the meat is falling-off-the-bone tender and the yucca has partially dissolved, leaving behind meltingly soft nubbins with a pleasing, slightly gummy texture.

Using tongs or a slotted spoon, remove the thigh and place it on plate. Once it is cool enough to handle, remove the skin and bone (reserve both for bone stock) and cut or tear the meat into bite-size pieces. Return the turkey to the soup, add the oregano, and reheat if needed. Add the lime juice. Taste; if it's too sour, add more salt. Spoon into bowls, garnish with avocado, and serve.

Mexican Oregano: An Invaluable Herb for South-of-the-Border Soups and Stews

Mexican oregano (*Lippia graveolens*), also known as Puerto Rican oregano, is a member of lemon verbena family and grows as a shrub or small tree throughout Central and South America. Its taste is similar to a vibrant savory with citrusy and licorice-like flavors, and it is widely valued for its culinary and medicinal uses; the latter includes antiviral and antimicrobial properties. The more common Mediterranean oregano (*Origanum vulgare*) is a member of the mint family.

Fresh Mexican oregano has some availability in regional markets and it is easily cultivated from seed or cuttings. Dried Mexican oregano is readily available in Western, Southwestern, Mexican, and international markets as well as online.

Wild Rice, Gigante Bean, and Amphissa Olive Soup

It's with good reason that cuisines from all hemispheres combine rice and beans in a wholesome one-dish meal. For such a soup that's bold, we meld our most robustly flavored grain, wild rice, with flavors from the mountains of central Greece. Ripe, purplish black amphissa olives lend both sweetness and tang to this soup. While creamy smooth Greek gigante beans are becoming increasingly available, lima or another large white bean works well (but not the pickled and canned gigante beans).

If possible, use traditionally harvested wild rice from a reservation, such as Leach Lake, for the most complex flavor profile (paddy-grown rice has a limited gene profile and less complex flavor than canoe-harvested wild rice). This recipe calls for precooked wild rice. As the cooking time and liquid measurement for wild rice varies considerably depending upon how it was grown and processed, your best bet is to follow the package directions. To make a thicker, stewlike soup, precook the wild rice with 1½ times the amount of liquid (for example, if 2 cups liquid are called for, add 3 cups liquid) and increase the cooking time by 15 minutes, or until the grains start to "butterfly," or split open.

Should you have any cooking liquid left over from the rice, add it to the soup in place of some of the stock for its rich flavor and added nutrients. This soup is even better the second day.

SERVES 6

- 1 pimiento or red bell pepper, roasted (see page 67) and diced
- 1 peperoncino, yellow wax, or yellow bell pepper, roasted (see page 67) and diced
- 1 tablespoon red wine vinegar
- 5 tablespoons extra-virgin olive oil, preferably Greek
- Unrefined salt and freshly ground black pepper
- 1 red onion, diced
- 1 carrot, thinly sliced
- 2 fennel bulbs, cored and chopped
- 2 cups cooked wild rice
- 1 cup cooked Greek gigante, lima, mortgage lifter, or great northern beans (see page 73), drained
- 6 cups stock (pages 5–10) or water
- 12 ripe amphissa or kalamata olives, pitted and sliced
- 2 tablespoons minced fresh oregano
- 2 teaspoons minced fresh savory, thyme, or rosemary
- 2 tablespoons chopped fennel fronds (optional)

In a medium bowl or container, combine the peppers, vinegar, and 2 tablespoons of the oil. Season with salt and pepper, stir well to coat the peppers, cover, and refrigerate for 8 hours or overnight.

Heat the remaining 3 tablespoons of oil in a large saucepan over medium heat. Add the onion, carrot, and fennel and sauté for 5 minutes, or until softened. Add the wild rice, beans, and stock. Bring to a simmer, cover, then reduce the heat and simmer for 5 to 7 minutes to combine the flavors. Drain the peppers, reserving their marinade for another use, such as in a salad dressing, and add the peppers to the soup. Stir in the olives, oregano, and savory and simmer for 5 minutes. Taste and adjust the seasoning with salt and pepper if needed. Spoon into bowls, drizzle with additional oil, garnish with the fennel fronds, if using, and serve.

Easy-to-Digest Beans

Bean soup is perhaps a more universal image of nurture than is a loaf of bread. Unpretentious, filling, and warming, a bean, pea, or lentil soup simmering on the back of the stove evokes home cooking at its humble best.

For most people well-cooked beans are easy to digest, but as that's not everyone's experience, here are three steps to maximize their digestibility.

Add ingredients that support digestion: A bowl of 100 percent beans would sit heavy on even the heartiest of tummies. But add a variety of vegetables, salt, a rich broth, herbs that enhance digestion, and oil or fat, as we do in the bean-based recipes in this book, and you'll not only have a great soup but one that goes down easy. If beans are relatively new to your diet or if you have trouble digesting them, start by eating small amounts frequently to allow your digestive system time to adjust to them. You may also try taking a bean-digestive enzyme supplement, such as Beano.

Figure out which varieties suit you best: Some folks most easily digest dal (any variety of hulled and split beans). And while lentils are easy for some, for others it might be any of the large common bean family (including pinto, red, and cannellini beans), or the *vigna* family beans (including aduki beans, black-eyed peas, and mung beans).

Toss the soaking and cooking water: Whether they're from a can or home cooked, it's important that both the bean-soaking water and cooking water are discarded, for doing so eliminates their hard-to-digest galactans (a type of carbohydrate).

A Simple Pot of Beans

MAKES 2 TO 3 CUPS COOKED BEANS

1 cup dried beans, picked over and rinsed	1 teaspoon unrefined salt
1 (2-inch) strip kombu (optional)	

Place the beans in a bowl, add water to cover by a few inches, and soak for 2 to 24 hours, until fully hydrated. Drain and rinse thoroughly.

Place the beans in a large saucepan, add fresh water to cover and the kombu, if using. Place over high heat and bring to a simmer, skimming off and discarding any foam that rises to the top. Reduce the heat and simmer until the beans are softened (cooking time varies greatly among different varieties), adding salt during the last 10 minutes of cooking. Drain and discard the cooking water and quickly rinse.

Mahi Mahi Moqueca

Rebecca's favorite restaurant is Pangea in Ashland, Oregon. Year after year Pangea garners Ashland's Best Soup accolade, and although its policy is to not give out recipes, being the owner's mother has its perks.

This classic Brazilian fish stew relies on red palm oil (a signature ingredient throughout the Amazon basin) for its golden hue (but it's equally tasty made with coconut oil if palm oil is unavailable) and the fish and coconut milk for their creamy sweetness and rich flavor. If mahi mahi is not local to your area, substitute any other white fish, such as halibut or bass. Serve over quinoa.

SERVES 4

1½ pounds mahi mahi, cut into 2-inch strips	¼ teaspoon cayenne pepper, or ½ teaspoon red pepper flakes, or to taste
2 tablespoons fresh lime juice, plus more for finishing the soup	½ teaspoon dried thyme
Unrefined salt	¼ teaspoon ground cinnamon
2 tablespoons unrefined red palm oil or coconut oil	3 medium yellow potatoes, cut into 1½-inch cubes
1 large onion, chopped	1 cup chopped tomatoes
1½ cups sliced light-colored mushrooms, such as oyster, chanterelle, or hedgehog	4 cups Vegetable Stock (page 8), Kombu-Shiitake Stock (page 9), or water
2 garlic cloves, minced	4 heads bok choy, leaves and stems kept separate, chopped
2 teaspoons cumin seeds	1 cup coconut milk
1½ teaspoons anise seeds	½ cup chopped fresh cilantro
1 teaspoon ground coriander	

Place the fish in a medium bowl. Toss with the lime juice and 1 teaspoon of salt. Set aside while you prepare the soup base.

Heat the oil in a large sauté pan or Dutch oven over medium heat. Add the onion, mushrooms, and garlic and sauté for about 5 minutes, until softened. Add the cumin seeds, anise seeds, coriander, cayenne, thyme, and cinnamon and sauté for an additional 5 minutes.

Add the potatoes, tomatoes, and stock, bring to a boil, then reduce the heat, cover the pan, and simmer for about 15 minutes, until the potatoes are cooked through. Add the fish and cook until just barely cooked through, about 5 minutes, more or less depending on how thick the cut is. Stir in the bok choy stems and cook for 1 minute. Add the coconut milk and cook for about 1 minute to heat through; take care that the soup does not boil after you've added the coconut milk so the coconut milk doesn't separate. Turn off the heat. Stir in the bok choy leaves and cilantro, add lime juice to taste, and adjust the seasoning with salt and pepper. Carefully ladle the soup into shallow bowls so as to not break the fish. Serve immediately.

What Makes Coconut Milk "Light"?

When choosing coconut milk from a can or box, pass on the "light" option. The light version costs the same but is made from a second extraction and so contains less flavor and nutrition; it may also contain a thickener, the identity of which may or may not be listed on the label. So if you'd like to lighten up your coconut milk—and stretch your food dollar—simply add some water to regular coconut milk.

Spanish Chickpea and Spinach Stew

Stew doesn't have to be a long-cooking affair to provide its comfort food appeal, as in this dish that takes under thirty minutes from pan to bowl. It's great twelve months of the year, and packed into a thermos it becomes a substantial meal away from home. Using baby spinach makes for an easy way of enjoying your greens, as it often comes prewashed and ready to go without additional prep, but if your garden is boasting another tender green such as chard, mizuna, or radish, turnip, or daikon tops, by all means, favor what's at hand. An equal amount of raisins can be substituted for the dates, if you like.

SERVES 4 TO 6

5	dried dates	1	cup stock (pages 5–10) or water, or as needed
	Pinch of saffron	3	cups cooked, drained chickpeas (see page 73), or 2 (15-ounce) cans, rinsed and drained
2	tablespoons extra-virgin olive oil, plus more for drizzling	1	medium tomato, chopped, or ½ cup canned diced tomatoes
1	medium onion, finely chopped	1	teaspoon unrefined salt, or to taste
2	garlic cloves, finely chopped	¼	teaspoon freshly ground black pepper
1	tablespoon sweet paprika	8	ounces baby spinach
¼	teaspoon ground cumin		Rice or another whole grain or cornbread (page 107), for serving
	Pinch of ground cinnamon		
	Pinch of freshly grated nutmeg		

Place the dates in a medium bowl, add hot water to cover, and leave for 30 minutes to soften. Drain, then pit and chop the dates. While the dates are soaking, place the saffron in a small bowl or teacup, add 1 tablespoon of hot water, and leave to bloom for at least 15 minutes, or until you're ready to proceed with the recipe.

In a large sauté pan, heat the oil over medium heat. Add the onion and sauté until softened, about 5 minutes. Add the garlic and sauté for 2 minutes. Add the paprika, cumin, cinnamon, and nutmeg and cook, stirring, for about 1 minute, until aromatic.

Add the stock and stir to release any browned bits from the bottom of the pan, then add the chickpeas, tomato, dates, saffron, salt, and pepper. Bring to a simmer, then reduce the heat a little and simmer for about 15 minutes, until thickened, adding more stock if the pan starts to dry.

Increase the heat to medium-high and add the spinach by the handful, stirring to wilt each addition. When all the spinach is added and wilted, the stew is done. Taste and adjust the seasonings with salt and pepper, if needed. Serve over rice or another grain or with a wedge of cornbread alongside.

Mom's Navy Bean Soup with Bacon

As a child, Rebecca's favorite thing about dining on ham was anticipating the sure-to-follow navy bean soup cooked with the ham bone. She clearly recalls her mother sitting at the Formica table before a small mound of navy beans, culling the rejects. It's a timeless image. Indeed, fingering your way through a cup of beans takes but a minute and is an opportunity to feel at one with all cooks past and future.

Don't be stingy when it comes to adding the bacon drippings to the soup. Here's why: Energetically beans are considered a dry and heavy food that is hard to digest, and therefore "windy." In addition to upping the flavor, fat quells wind and it lubricates the beans so that they don't sit so heavy. You can get a sense of this by recalling the many rich-in-fat traditional bean dishes, such as refried beans, bean fritters, and hummus. Or, conversely, try to imagine a fat-free hummus with neither olive oil nor tahini.

By using preservative-free bacon, a bone stock, and the bacon drippings, this replication is free of the sodium nitrate found in commercial hams and is as full-flavored as one using a ham bone or hock.

SERVES 4 TO 6

8	ounces preservative-free bacon
1	onion, diced
2	celery stalks, chopped
1	large carrot, chopped
½	teaspoon ground cumin
¼ to ½	teaspoon red pepper flakes
1	bay leaf
3	cups cooked navy or great white northern beans (see page 73), or 2 (15-ounce) cans, drained and rinsed
4	cups stock (pages 5–10)
	Unrefined salt
2	tablespoons chopped fresh chives

Tasty Lunch Options

If more often than you wish to recall you have settled for an overpriced and not-so-satisfying lunch, here's a pleasurable option. Make a one-time purchase of a good thermos, pack up any one of our delicious soups or stews in it, and you're set. For gluten and dairy-free folks, exercising the thermos option is a particularly invaluable strategy.

What about joining others at a restaurant? Depending upon circumstances and what options the restaurant offers, you might order a salad, ask for a bowl, decant some of Mom's Navy Bean Soup with Bacon (page 78) or another substantial soup into it, and feast on your own terms. When breaking bread with others and yours is gluten and dairy free, offer to share. When others at table are also nibbling on your Almond and Flax Crackers (page 108) or Cornbread (page 107), you'll all feel a sense of connection and community.

Put the bacon in a large skillet and add enough water to cover the bottom of the pan. Place over medium-high heat and cook until the water has evaporated, about 8 minutes. Reduce the heat to medium-low and cook until the bacon is crisp, another 5 minutes or so, turning the slices a couple of times. Transfer to a plate and set aside. Strain the bacon drippings into a glass measuring cup and reserve.

Heat ⅓ cup of the reserved bacon fat (if your bacon rendered less than ⅓ cup of fat, you can supplement with lard, unrefined coconut oil, or extra-virgin olive oil) in a medium saucepan over medium heat. Add the onion and sauté for about 3 minutes, until translucent. Add the celery, carrot, cumin, and chile flakes and sauté for about 3 minutes, until the vegetables start to soften. Add the bay leaf, beans, and stock and season with salt, keeping in mind the bacon will add some extra saltiness. Bring to a boil, then reduce the heat and simmer, uncovered, for 15 minutes.

Crumble the bacon and reserve some for a garnish; stir the rest into the soup and cook for an additional 5 minutes to soften the bacon. Remove the bay leaf. Divide into bowls, garnish with the chives and the remaining bacon, and serve.

Quinoa Kabocha Pottage

When quinoa was introduced to North America by Steve Gorad and Don McKinley in 1983, the two men asked Rebecca to develop recipes for this heretofore unavailable grain. Rebecca, gladly obliging, traveled to the altiplano for research and published the first book on the subject in English, *Quinoa: The Supergrain*. Of the book's 120 recipes, this simple stew remains her favorite.

Quinoa and squash combine to make a perfect pottage (thick vegetable soup). While many recipes call for butternut squash, we favor the more earthy sweetness and bright orange flesh of kabocha squash (also known as Hokkaido pumpkin); this squash has either gray-blue or orange skin and is round like a small pumpkin but with a slightly elongated, teardrop-shaped top). Buttercup and butternut squash also work, but pass on the less flavorful turban, spaghetti, or acorn squash for this soup.

There's no need to peel the squash; simply trim any tough or warty spots from it. If you use a green-skinned squash, the small flecks of green will add both an attractive color and nutrients to the stew.

SERVES 4

2	tablespoons extra-virgin olive oil		2	cups chopped kabocha squash
1	teaspoon cumin seeds		½	cup uncooked quinoa
1	onion, chopped		4	cups stock (pages 5–10)
1	celery stalk, chopped		1	teaspoon unrefined salt
1	teaspoon ground allspice		2	sprigs thyme, or ½ teaspoon dried thyme
¼	teaspoon red pepper flakes, or to taste		1	scallion, minced

Heat the oil in a large saucepan over medium heat; add the cumin seeds and sauté for 1 minute, or until aromatic. Add the onion and sauté for 3 to 5 minutes, until softened. Add the celery, allspice, pepper flakes, and squash and cook for about 5 minutes, until the surface of the squash starts to soften. Add the quinoa, stock, salt, and thyme and bring to a boil. Reduce the heat, cover, and simmer for 15 minutes, or until the squash is softened.

With five to ten strokes of a potato masher or ricer, puree most of the squash to create a stewlike consistency. Adjust the seasonings and remove the thyme sprigs, if you used them. Spoon into bowls, garnish with the scallion, and serve.

A Stash of Squash

We save this recipe for after the first good frost and through February, when local winter squash is at its prime and most economical and plentiful. The flavor of the imported squash that's available in warmer months is so thin that it's almost a safer bet to substitute canned unseasoned pumpkin than hazard buying it. While some people might use frozen squash chunks, another option would be to substitute carrots and wait for seasonal squash. If you're lucky enough to have a root cellar, you can store local squash until early spring. If you don't have a root cellar, put a stash in a garage or under a bed or in the bottom shelf of a dresser in an unheated guest room. Store squash so that they are not touching, cover with newspapers or a blanket for insulation, and as you slowly work through your supply, first select out and use up any that develop a soft spot.

Hearty Sweet Potato and Celeriac Soup with Sausage Bites

The sweetly piquant flavor of celery root plus the smooth sweetness of sweet potato and punchy sausage flavors make a homey and hearty soup. For a light touch, we add the bok choy just at the end and dish the soup up while the bok choy stems still have a slight crunch; this contrasts nicely with the smoothness of the yam and meatiness of the sausage.

The recipe calls for uncooked sausage bites that poach in the simmering stock; to kick up the flavor a notch, lightly brown the sausage in a skillet, draining excess fat (or not) before adding the bites to the soup.

SERVES 4 AS A STARTER OR 2 AS A MEAL

2	tablespoons extra-virgin olive oil		6	cups stock (pages 5–10) or water
1	teaspoon cumin seeds		1	teaspoon unrefined salt, or to taste
1	leek, white and light green parts (save the greens for stock), cleaned and chopped			Freshly ground black pepper
1	small to medium celeriac, peeled and cut into 1-inch cubes (about 2 cups)		12	ounces ground loose pastured sausage meat
			2	tablespoons minced fresh chives or cilantro
1	large sweet potato, peeled and cut into 1-inch cubes		1 to 2	heads baby bok choy, chopped (about 3 cups)

Heat the oil in a large saucepan and add the cumin; cook until aromatic, 2 to 3 minutes. Add the leek and celeriac and sauté for about 5 minutes, until softened. Add the sweet potato and stock and season with the salt and pepper. Bring to a boil, then reduce the heat and simmer for 10 to 15 minutes, until the vegetables are tender.

Meanwhile, combine the sausage with 1 tablespoon of the chives and season with salt and pepper; mix to thoroughly incorporate and form the mixture into 1-inch bites. Add the sausage bites to the soup and cook for 2 to 3 minutes, until cooked through. Add the bok choy and simmer for 1 to 2 minutes, until just lightly cooked but still crisp. Divide the soup among bowls and garnish with the remaining 1 tablespoon chives.

Up the Texture, Up the Pleasure

There's something soothing about a thick and creamy soup, and with good reason; aside from the comfort food appeal, when that soup is gluten and dairy free it literally soothes an irritated digestive system. And perhaps you've noticed how a soup with substance tends to better quell mental stress or fatigue than does a thin soup. Here are some of our favorite gluten- and dairy-free ways to thicken a soup:

Include Potatoes or Other Starchy Vegetables

Cook potatoes into the soup and blend, as for the Puree of Asparagus with Dill (page 60) and Radish-Top Soup with Salted Radishes (page 57).

Favor russets; while cooking draws the starch from any potato and so lends body to a soup, the starch in russet potatoes dissolves most quickly and fully and lends a creamier texture. Try russets in place of yellow potatoes anywhere they're called for, as in the Mahi Mahi Moqueca (page 74), Gulyás (page 96), or Orange and Saffron Fish Stew (page 100).

Add yucca; its starch naturally thickens a soup, as in the Yucatán Turkey Thigh and Yucca Soup (page 68).

Add Grains or Legumes

Cook a little rice into the soup and blend, as for the Carrot Soup with Garlic Chips (page 48), or make long-cooked rice the base for your soup, as we do with Congee Five Ways (page 92).

Blend beans, as for the Cream of Fava Soup with Cumin, Mint, and Salt-Preserved Lemon (page 54), or cook lentils until they start to fall apart, as for the Smoky Split Yellow Pea Soup with Spinach and Lime (page 41).

Add chickpea flour instead of standard wheat flour, as for the Mulligatawny Soup (page 58).

Make a roux based on rice flour rather than all-purpose flour, as for the Shrimp and Sausage Étouffée (page 98).

Add Nuts or Fruit

Add coconut milk, as in the Cream of Mushroom Soup (page 44), Cream of Tomato and Beet Soup (page 62), and Mahi Mahi Moqueca (page 74).

Blend in an avocado, as we do for the Minty Avocado and Tomatillo Soup (page 51).

Add Cashew Sour Cream (page 103), as for the Cultured White Gazpacho (page 43).

Blend, Mash, or Puree It

Blend part or all of the soup, as for the Cream of Mushroom Soup (page 44) and Puree of Asparagus with Dill (page 60).

Mash part of the soup, using a potato masher, as we do with the Quinoa Kabocha Potage (page 80).

Poach whole garlic cloves in olive oil and puree them into the soup, as for the Leek and Scallion Soup with Garlic Cream (page 52).

Slow-Cooker Pork Tinga (Mexican Shredded Pork Stew)

This popular Mexican stew, based on our favorite smoky chile, the chipotle, is serious comfort food: pork cooked low and slow in a spicy tomato-based sauce with hearty collard greens added at the end to sop up the flavorful juices. We're liberal with our chipotles here, making this tinga spicy; to tone down the heat, use half a can or even just one chipotle for the mildest tastes.

Set up your tinga before you go to work, and when you get home warm a tortilla or two and kick back with a bowlful. Or start it before you go to bed and enjoy it as a superhearty breakfast, with leftovers for your lunchbox.

SERVES 6 TO 8

1	tablespoon lard, virgin coconut oil, or extra-virgin olive oil
3½ to 4	pounds boneless pastured pork shoulder, cut into 1-inch cubes
1	(28-ounce) can whole tomatoes
2	medium white onions, sliced
3	garlic cloves, chopped
1	(7-ounce) can chipotle chiles in adobo sauce, chopped
1½	teaspoons dried oregano
1½	teaspoons unrefined salt
2	bunches collard greens, stemmed and cut into chiffonade (see sidebar), then chopped
	Accompaniments: Rice or 100% corn tortillas, and sliced avocado, red onion, and radishes

Chipotle Chiles

Chipotle chiles are dried, smoked jalapeños that add a distinctly smoky flavor to any dish they're added to. Canned chipotle chiles in adobo sauce (a vinegar-based sauce) can be found in most supermarkets in the Latino foods section. Read the labels, as some brands contain wheat, in the form of wheat starch.

Heat the oil in a large skillet or sauté pan over medium-high heat. Add half of the pork and brown it all over, stirring a few times, about 10 minutes. Transfer the pork to a slow cooker. Add the remaining pork to the skillet and brown it in the same way. Transfer the remaining pork to the slow cooker. Pour about ¼ cup of the tomato juices from the can into the skillet and stir to release any browned bits from the bottom of the skillet. Pour the liquid over the pork.

Add the onions, garlic, chipotle chiles with their sauce, oregano, and salt to the slow cooker. Crush the tomatoes directly into the pot. No need to stir.

Cover and cook for about 6 hours on high or 12 hours on low, until the meat is fall-apart tender. Mash the pork with a potato masher; it should break apart easily. Stir in the collards, cover, and cook for 20 minutes. Spoon out some of the fat at the top of the slow cooker if you like.

Serve over rice or with corn tortillas, with avocado, red onion, and radishes. If you're making tacos, scoop the tinga out with a slotted spoon to keep your tortillas from getting soggy.

How to Chiffonade

Chiffonade is a method of cutting leafy herbs or green vegetables into long, thin strips. In French *chiffon* means "rag," so to chiffonade is to turn your greens into raglike strips. For the collard greens in this recipe, the strips are then chopped so they're easier to eat with the stew.
1. Remove the stems from your herb or vegetable.
2. Evenly stack a few leaves lengthwise in front of you.
3. Using your fingertips, grab of the edge of the stack closest to you and roll up the leaves into a tight bundle.
4. Use a sharp knife to cut the bundle crosswise into thin, even strips, then gently separate the strips.

Tibetan Thukpa

Over the years, Rebecca has enjoyed cooking for traditional Tibetan teachers, and 365 days of the year, supper is the same comforting one-dish meal. Thukpa is that delicious! This no-fuss soup takes its name from the hand-pulled noodle it contains, and in some dialects the term *thukpa* also means "dinner." Long simmering extracts the essence from bones and tenderizes an inexpensive cut of meat to yield this energizing and deeply satisfying meal. Use beef, mutton, lamb, or more traditionally, yak meat.

It's aboveboard to pick out a bone from your bowl to gnaw on. After all, meat next to the bone is the most flavorful, and there's something gratifying about working a bone. If there's a marrow bone in the pot, the guest of honor receives it. Ladle a bone into each serving and place empty saucers on the table for the remainders; include a steak knife alongside the spoon at each place setting as well.

The traditional hand-pulled noodle is made from wheat dough that's stretched into a long, thick rope that's dangled over one arm while pieces are rapidly pinched off and dropped into the soup. Our thukpa uses mung bean pasta because it's wheat free and its overall effect is cooling and helps moderate the soup's heartiness. You could also use a packaged gluten-free pasta of your choice. As many gluten-free pastas made from grains tend to dissolve into a soup, it's best to cook the pasta separately and then combine it with the soup in individual bowls.

SERVES 4 TO 6

3 dried shiitake mushrooms	1 tablespoon minced fresh ginger
2½ pounds (4-inch) pastured short ribs, cross-cut shanks, or other meat on the bone (see headnote)	1½ teaspoons unrefined salt
2 tablespoons extra-virgin olive oil	1 daikon, trimmed, quartered lengthwise, and chopped into ½-inch pieces (about 3 cups)
1 large onion, chopped	4 ounces mung bean pasta (vermicelli)
2 garlic cloves, chopped	3 heads baby bok choy, chopped (about 3 cups)
2 jalapeño chiles, seeded and diced	4 scallions, white and green parts, chopped
½ teaspoon ground Sichuan peppercorns (optional)	Asian-style hot sauce of choice (optional)

Soak the mushrooms in about ½ cup of warm water, just enough to cover, for about 30 minutes while you start the soup.

Trim any excess fat from the surface of the meat.

Heat 1 tablespoon of the oil in a large skillet over medium-high heat. Add the meat and brown it on all sides, turning as necessary, for about 20 minutes. You may partially cover the skillet to prevent sputtering oil.

Meanwhile, heat 1 tablespoon of the remaining oil in a large saucepan over medium heat. Add the onion and garlic and sauté for about 5 minutes, until softened. Add the daikon, jalapeños, Sichuan pepper, if using, and the ginger and sauté until the vegetables are starting to soften, about 5 minutes. Add the salt, the browned meat, and enough water to cover the ingredients.

Strain the mushrooms, reserving their soaking water. Slice the mushrooms (if the stems remain hard, discard them or reserve them for stock making) and add both the shiitakes and their soaking water. Increase the heat to high and bring to a boil; reduce the heat and simmer, uncovered, for 5 minutes, skimming off any surface foam that forms. Reduce the heat to the lowest setting, cover, and simmer for 2 to 3 hours, until the meat nearly falls off the bone, adding more water if necessary to keep the meat covered and adding the daikon about 15 minutes before the soup is ready. Spoon off any excess fat from the soup's surface, if you like.

Meanwhile, prepare the pasta: Place it in a small saucepan, add warm water to cover, and soak for about 5 minutes, until it softens. Turn the heat to high, bring to a simmer, then reduce the heat and simmer for 3 to 5 minutes, just until the pasta becomes uniformly translucent. Drain. Using kitchen shears or a butter knife, cut into any length you like and divide the pasta into four bowls.

Add the bok choy to the soup and simmer for 3 minutes, or until tender. Stir in the scallions and remove from the heat. Spoon the soup into the bowls and serve with hot sauce to pass at the table, if you like.

Slumgullion

This no-fuss, no-frills Irish-American stew was popular through the 1950s and a welcome standby on family camping trips when Rebecca was a child, for it was as easy and unpretentious as browning hamburger, adding a can of diced tomatoes and some macaroni, and simmering until the pasta was cooked. Its name has a great ring to it, and the stew itself is both substantial and satisfying, especially with the simple upgrades that mushrooms and a chile add, and, for its tang and a touch of the Irish, flakes of dulse. Served alongside a salad and crackers, slumgullion makes an excellent one-pot meal.

SERVES 4 TO 6

1	tablespoon red palm oil or extra-virgin olive oil
1	pound pastured ground beef
1	onion, chopped
1	cup chopped mushrooms
1	New Mexico or poblano chile, roasted (see page 67), or 1 unroasted jalapeño or serrano chile, chopped
2	cups peeled, seeded, and chopped tomatoes, or 1 (15-ounce) can chopped tomatoes
1	teaspoon unrefined salt
2	cups stock (pages 5–10) or water, or more if needed
8	ounces gluten-free elbows, shells, or macaroni (about 2 cups dried pasta)
2	tablespoons dulse flakes
	Freshly ground black pepper
¼	cup chopped fresh cilantro

Heat the oil in a large saucepan over medium heat. Add the ground beef and, with a spatula, press it out to cover the surface of the pan. Increase the heat to medium-high and brown the beef for about 7 minutes, until the meat shrinks a little and the bottom is browned. Turn and brown the other side for about 5 minutes. Using a spatula, break the meat into pieces and slide to one side of the pan. Add the onion, mushrooms, and chile to the other side of the pan and sauté for about 5 minutes, until the vegetables are softened.

Add the tomatoes, salt, and stock and bring to a boil. Add the pasta and dulse, reduce the heat to a high simmer, and cook for about 10 minutes, just until the pasta is cooked to al dente; take care to not overcook the pasta and add more stock if the mixture starts to dry. Season with pepper, taste, and adjust the seasoning, if needed. Stir in the cilantro, spoon into bowls, and serve.

Browning Meat for the Soup Pot: Why It's Worth the Extra Step

Although browning meat is an extra step, it's well worth the effort. In addition to giving your soup a richer eye appeal, browning or searing brings out wondrous and multifaceted flavors and aromas unachievable in a soup pot alone. Here's why.

A minimum temperature of 230°F is required for the chemical reactions needed to turn the surface of a food brown (the Maillard reaction); foods cooked at a lower temperature can't brown. For example, because water or stock can't exceed the boiling point (212°F), boiled white rice stays white. Unless, that is, you overcook it, for when all the water is absorbed, the temperature increases above the boiling point and the bottom of that white rice becomes golden—and oh so delicious—then brown and (whoops!) eventually black.

To brown meat, fill a sauté pan no more than two-thirds full with meat, for if the meat is crowded, juices will collect rather than evaporate and the meat will stew rather than brown. If necessary, brown the meat in two batches rather than overcrowding the pan. Partially cover the pan (but don't fully cover it, as again the meat will stew rather than brown) to reduce sputtering, or use a splatter shield and consider wearing a bib apron.

As searing meat invites a medium-high heat, we recommend using fat that healthfully withstands higher temperatures, such as lard, schmaltz (chicken fat), coconut oil, or red palm oil. Lard and bacon drippings are rich in umami and so treble the flavor of other ingredients. That being said, as the omega-9 fatty acids in olive oil healthfully withstand temperatures as high as 325°F, it is possible to brown meat using olive oil; if you do so, take care to cook it at a more moderate temperature. For more on oils for sautéing, see page 46–47.

May Day Stew

If you think that stew is strictly a cold-weather dish, surprise yourself otherwise! This gorgeous spring stew features tender veggies at their flavor peak to reveal their unadulterated essence. The taters and turnips become earthy-sweet, and the colorful green asparagus and peas become brighter. This winsome dish is a light and satisfying first course.

To make the most of those treasured first vegetables of the season, dedicate this soup to spring. But the cooking technique—blanching vegetables individually and combining them at the end—works with vegetables from any season: for example, cabbage, fennel, carrots, daikon, bok choy, bean sprouts, broccoli, broccolini, radishes, and cauliflower.

This recipe makes perfect use of a pasta pot with a strainer insert: it enables cooking in—and removing each vegetable from—the insert. Or cook the vegetables in a large pot and remove them with a slotted spoon or a spider (a wide, shallow wire-mesh basket with a long handle).

Note: To retain the vibrant colors of the blanched vegetables, use a wide skillet or wok to quickly heat the soup.

SERVES 4

1	tablespoon plus 1 teaspoon unrefined salt
8	ounces purple fingerling or new potatoes, cut into chunks
4	baby turnips, trimmed and cut in half or quartered if large
12	ounces asparagus, woody ends discarded (save them for soup stock) and chopped
2	cups snow peas, stem ends removed and cut in half
4	scallions, chopped
3	sprigs fresh tarragon or savory
	Freshly ground black pepper
1	tablespoon fresh lemon juice
¼	cup unrefined hazelnut oil or extra-virgin olive oil

Bring 3 quarts water to a boil in a large saucepan; add 1 tablespoon of salt and the potatoes. Cook for 10 minutes, or until fork-tender. Using a slotted spoon, remove the potatoes to a large bowl and set aside.

Repeat with the remaining vegetables, separately blanching the turnips, asparagus, and then the snow peas until each is just cooked and adding them to the bowl. Reserve 2 cups of the blanching water.

Place the scallions, two tarragon sprigs, and the blanching water in a wide skillet or wok (a wide vessel makes for quicker heating and you retain the vibrant colors of the blanched vegetables).

Add the vegetables and heat just until they're warmed through. Add the lemon juice and the remaining 1 teaspoon of salt and season with pepper; simmer for 1 minute. Mince the remaining tarragon.

Divide the stew among bowls, garnish with the minced tarragon, drizzle each bowl with hazelnut oil, and serve hot.

Note: Once you've made this soup a time or two, here's a shortcut: When the potatoes are close to being done, add the turnips, cook briefly, and then add the next ingredient, and so on. You start with the vegetable that requires the most cooking and end with the vegetable that requires the least, and at the end when you drain the whole pot each vegetable each will be cooked just right.

Congee Five Ways

ongee, also known as *jook, okayu, kanji, kichadi,* or *bubur,* depending upon the region, is a long-cooked, thick rice soup that is a breakfast staple throughout Asia. While congee variations are legion, it always consists of a grain—typically rice—cooked with enough liquid and time for the grain to become porridgelike and easy to digest. I favor white rice, as it yields a creamy, smooth texture, but you may readily substitute brown rice.

Congee is easy to make in a slow cooker. Put up the soup before going to bed and awaken to this satisfying porridge. (Or put it up before going to work and the soup will be ready when you come home.)

SERVES 2

½	cup uncooked white rice
4	cups water
1	(2-inch) piece kombu seaweed
1	bay leaf
1	teaspoon minced fresh ginger
½	teaspoon unrefined salt
¼	teaspoon ground cumin
1	chicken thigh on the bone

Possible garnishes: chopped scallions, crisp fried onions or Garlic Chips (page 48), bamboo shoots, chili sauce

Place all the ingredients except the garnishes in a large saucepan. Bring to a boil over medium-high heat, then reduce the heat to the very lowest and cook for at least 3 hours or up to 8 hours. (Or cook in a slow cooker on low for about 8 hours.) Add additional water if necessary. Remove the chicken bone, adjust the seasoning to taste, and garnish with your choice of toppings.

Congee as Traditional Chinese Medicine

To elevate congee above its already soothing and healing soup profile, add ingredients targeted to your specific health needs. These five variations can tailor your congee to what your body is calling for at any time. For more ideas, see *The Book of Jook: Chinese Medicinal Porridges—A Healthy Alternative to the Typical Western Breakfast* by Bob Flaws.

Kidney Tonic: Cook with ½ cup of raw peanuts.

Lung Tonic: Cook with a sliced lotus root.

Flu or Cold Tonic (not with a fever): Cook with ½ diced yam and, for the last 5 minutes of cooking, 1 cup of chopped mustard greens.

Energy Tonic: Substitute beef shanks for the chicken thigh; garnish with shredded romaine lettuce.

Immune Tonic: Cook with three reconstituted dried shiitake mushrooms; garnish with julienned ginger.

Posole with Lamb

Posole (lime-slaked corn), the quintessential Southwestern grain, so excels in soup that the term *posole* refers to both the grain and the soup of the same. Posole is available in Latino sections of supermarkets and natural food stores and online. For the best flavor, use dried rather than frozen or canned posole (also known as hominy).

Rebecca was once the guest of the Deer Clan matriarch in the Zuni pueblo and feasted on this soup. The men and some older boys of that clan, after having done a strenuous daylong annual pilgrimage—many of them barefoot—to their sacred salt mine, then danced continuously from dusk to dawn and broke fast with this sustaining dish. After they started dancing, an aproned elder with long, graying braids and a cotton print bib apron oversaw us as we placed three 5-gallon pots of posole and mutton in the juniper embers of an outdoor earthen horno. Her six-year-old great-great-granddaughter, in a brightly embroidered apron, was at her side. The elder helped seal the door, and the posole simmered through the night while the men danced on.

If you enjoy lamb, odds are you'll love long-cooked mutton, the meat of an adult sheep. Mutton has fallen out of favor, but ranchers and old-timers will tell you differently; our taste buds delight in this tender, deeply sweet, and complexly flavored meat. After you've made this recipe with lamb, try it with mutton, available in Latino markets, or if possible search out a local farm that can supply you; increase the cooking time for mutton by 1½ hours.

Two prerequisites for this dish are that the bones are cooked in the soup and that it's served with both salsa verde and roja (green and red salsa) for seasoning to your individual taste. You'll notice that this authentic recipe has only an onion and garlic for vegetables, and, as you'll discover, it needs no other embellishment. The recipe it was modeled after was served with flatbread, peas, salad, Jell-O, and an assortment of olives and pickles.

SERVES 6

1½	cups dried posole
2	(2-pound) pastured lamb shanks, each cut into 3 pieces
6	cups water
1	large onion, chopped
4	garlic cloves, chopped
	Unrefined salt
¼	cup chopped fresh oregano

Fresh lime juice

Freshly ground black pepper

Green and red prepared salsas, for serving

Soak the posole in water to cover for 4 to 8 hours.

Drain and discard the posole-soaking water, rinse the posole, and place it in a large saucepan. Add the lamb and water and bring to a boil over high heat. Reduce the heat and simmer for 5 minutes with the lid off. Skim off and discard the foam that forms at the surface, then add the onion, garlic, and salt to taste. Return the heat to a simmer, then cover and cook at a low simmer for 3 hours, or until both the posole and lamb are very tender; add more water if necessary. Skim off some of the fat that rises to the top; alternatively, let the soup cool, refrigerate, and scrape off the excess fat (lamb can be quite fatty, so this is recommended), then reheat the soup before serving.

Taste and adjust the seasonings if needed. Prior to serving, remove the shanks from the soup and remove the bones (optional: serve the bones on a separate plate for those who enjoy marrow). Cut the lamb into bite-size pieces or shred it, remove any gristle, and return the lamb pieces to the soup. Add the oregano and season with lime juice and pepper. Serve with the salsas.

Gulyás (Goulash)

Yu don't have to be Hungarian to appreciate the rich aroma and flavor of Hungary's national dish, gulyás. It's paprika, rather than tomatoes, that gives this stew its hallmark scarlet color and flavor. The amount of paprika might seem inordinate, but if you use less, expect a less wonderful result. If *very fresh* parsnips are available, they're perfect in this dish; otherwise use daikon and/or burdock. To elaborate on the Hungarian theme, serve with kasha, a salad or steamed green, and sauerkraut, and, for afters, a poached pear stuffed with chopped walnuts and crystallized ginger.

This stew requires a long simmer—that's what transforms the otherwise tough shanks into oh-so-tender bites. It's ready after 2½ hours of simmering on the stovetop, but sometimes we let it go for another hour or so. Or, for an even more melting texture and deeper flavor, place it in an enamel Dutch oven and bake in a 250°F oven all day or overnight. You may also make gulyás overnight in a slow cooker on low.

When serving gulyás family style, make sure there's a bone in each bowl and place plates on the table for the spent bones.

SERVES 4 TO 6

3 pounds pastured lamb shanks, cut into thirds, or cross-cut beef shanks or short ribs	2 carrots, chopped into large pieces
2 tablespoons red palm oil, lard, or extra-virgin olive oil	1 medium parsnip or small daikon or burdock, coarsely chopped
1 large onion, chopped	4 medium yellow potatoes, cut into 1½-inch cubes
6 garlic cloves, minced	1½ teaspoons unrefined salt, or to taste
2 teaspoons ground caraway	¼ cup sweet Hungarian paprika
4 ounces cremini or porcini mushrooms, sliced (about ½ cup)	1 to 3 teaspoons hot smoked paprika
	Cashew Sour Cream (page 103, optional)
	¼ cup chopped fresh flat-leaf parsley

Trim any extra fat from the lamb. Heat 1 tablespoon of the oil in a large sauté pan over medium-high heat. Add the lamb and brown it on all three sides, 20 to 25 minutes. You may partially cover the pan to avoid spattering, but do not cover the pan tightly or the meat will stew rather than brown.

Meanwhile, heat the remaining 1 tablespoon of oil in a large Dutch oven or heavy saucepan over medium heat. Add the onion and garlic and sauté for 5 to 7 minutes, until they are translucent. Add the caraway and mushrooms and sauté until the mushrooms soften and shrink, 4 to 5 minutes. Add the carrots and parsnip and cook for 4 to 5 minutes, until starting to soften.

Add the browned shanks—nestle them at the bottom of the pot—and the potatoes. Add enough water to partially cover the ingredients, then increase the heat to high and bring to a boil. Reduce the heat, partially cover, and simmer for 10 to 15 minutes, skimming off and discarding any brown foam from the surface. Add the sweet and hot smoked paprika, cover tightly, and simmer for 2½ hours or more, until very tender and falling off the bone. Taste and adjust the seasoning.

Using a slotted spoon, remove the larger shanks. The meat will be so tender that it breaks apart with a fork. Return the bone and meat to the stew. Or, prior to serving, use a slotted spoon to remove the shanks from the stew; when cool enough to handle, remove any large pieces of gristle and the bone, cut the meat into bite-size pieces, and return it to the stew. Taste and add a pinch or more salt if needed. Ladle the soup into bowls, garnish with sour cream, if you like, and the parsley, and serve.

Adapting a Recipe to Suit Your Whim

In our gulyás recipe, we call for browning the meat in a separate pan so that you can simultaneously sauté the vegetables in the Dutch oven. But stop and consider for a moment. Given this is the Hungarian national dish, try to imagine its countless variations and adaptations. So, knowing that long-simmered meat and veggies will turn out great no matter what, you can adapt this recipe to suit your time and preferences.

Try the one-pot method: Rather than using two pots as in the recipe directions, you may brown the meat in the Dutch oven, remove it, sauté the veggies, and then nestle the browned meat on top of the vegetables. Given how long it takes to brown the meat, this requires more time at the stove, but then there's only one pot to wash.

We've also made gulyás into a no-fuss, au blanc dish and bypassed the browning and sautéing steps: Simply combine all the ingredients in a pot and simmer away.

Shrimp and Sausage Étouffée

The word *étouffée* comes from the French word "to smother," and here shrimp and sausage are deliciously smothered in a Cajun- and Creole-style, roux-based gravy. A roux is a mixture of fat and flour, typically butter and white flour; here we swap in unrefined oil and rice flour for an equally tasty gluten- and dairy-free roux. Sweet rice flour, also known as glutinous rice flour, provides the best thickening power, but regular white rice flour will work as well. Both can be found in Asian grocery stores and some natural food stores.

In New Orleans you'll find this dish made with crawfish; try subbing in crawfish for the shrimp when you can find it. If the shrimp you picked up are in the shell, try making a stock with the shells to use in your étouffée: place the shells in a medium saucepan with a handful of any other vegetables and herbs you might have in your kitchen at the moment; add water to cover, bring to a boil, then reduce the heat, simmer for 45 minutes, strain, and use for your stock base.

SERVES 4

8	ounces andouille or other sausage, sliced		½	teaspoon freshly ground black pepper
3	tablespoons unrefined coconut oil, palm oil, lard, or other unrefined oil		½	teaspoon ground cayenne
¼	cup rice flour, preferably sweet rice flour (aka glutinous rice flour)		½	teaspoon dried oregano
			½	teaspoon dried thyme
1	large onion, chopped		1	medium tomato, chopped
1	large green bell pepper, chopped		1½	teaspoons unrefined salt, or to taste
1	cup chopped celery		2	cups stock (pages 5–10)
3	garlic cloves, minced		1	pound medium shrimp, peeled and deveined
1	teaspoon sweet paprika		2	tablespoons chopped fresh parsley
½	teaspoon garlic powder		¼	cup thinly sliced scallions
½	teaspoon onion powder			

Heat a large skillet over medium-high heat. Add the sausage and cook for about 10 minutes, turning once, until well browned on both sides. Transfer to a paper towel–lined plate and set aside.

In a large saucepan, heat the oil over medium heat until melted. Add the flour and stir constantly for about 25 minutes, until darkened to a brown roux (resembling the color of milk chocolate). Add the onion, bell peppers, celery, and garlic and cook, stirring frequently, until softened, about 10 minutes. Add the paprika, garlic powder, onion powder, black pepper, cayenne, oregano, and thyme and cook, stirring, for 2 minutes. Add the tomatoes and 1½ teaspoons of the salt, then whisk in the stock. Bring to a boil, then reduce the heat to low and simmer, stirring occasionally, for 25 minutes. Add the cooked sausage and cook for 10 minutes.

Place the shrimp in a bowl and toss with the remaining ½ teaspoon salt. Add to the pot and cook until cooked through, about 3 minutes. Add the parsley. Taste and adjust the seasonings if needed. Serve over rice or another grain and garnished with the scallions.

Orange and Saffron Fish Stew

This variation on Italian bouillabaisse, a rich, orangey-red stew, is brimming with fish and flavored with the floral notes of fennel, saffron, and orange. This beautiful recipe was shared with us by Leda's good friend and pastry chef Patricia Austin of Wild Flour Bakery of Vermont.

Including a variety of fish contributes to the stew's contrasting flavors and textures. Add more orange zest or juice for a bolder orange flavor, or include the orange blossom water for a subtle heightening of the stew's floral features. Saffron can vary in strength; adjust the amount according to taste. Serve in wide bowls, with a salad alongside to complete the meal.

SERVES 4 TO 6

3	pounds assorted fish and shellfish (see note)
⅓	cup extra-virgin olive oil
1	large yellow onion, chopped
5	large garlic cloves, minced
2	fennel bulbs, cored and thinly sliced, fronds reserved for garnish
	Leaves from 1 bunch flat-leaf parsley, finely chopped
2	(28-ounce) cans crushed tomatoes
1	quart Vegetable Stock (page 8)
5	medium unpeeled new potatoes, chopped
½	teaspoon saffron threads, or to taste
	Zest and juice of 1 large orange, or to taste
½	teaspoon orange blossom water (optional)
½	teaspoon unrefined salt

Cut the fish into 1-inch pieces (leave shellfish whole).

In a large saucepan, heat the oil over medium heat. Add the onion, garlic, fennel bulbs, and parsley and cook, uncovered, until the vegetables begin to soften, about 5 minutes. Add the tomatoes, stock, and potatoes and bring to a boil. Immediately reduce the heat and simmer until the broth has thickened into a stew consistency, about 45 minutes. Add the saffron threads, orange zest and juice, orange blossom water, if using, and salt and return to a simmer. Add firm-fleshed fish and cook for 5 minutes, then add tender-fleshed fish and shellfish, if using (see note), and cook for another 5 minutes, or until the fish are cooked through but still firm. Ladle into bowls, garnish with the reserved fennel fronds, and serve immediately.

Note: Include any fish you like—firm-fleshed fish, such as monkfish, swordfish, grouper, and halibut; and tender-fleshed fish, such as flounder, cod, and snapper (you can also include shellfish, such as scallops, lobster, and shrimp).

ACCOMPANIMENTS

Cashew Sour Cream

We've never been fans of ersatz ingredients or products that mimic traditionally dairy- or wheat-based foods via use of unwholesome substitutes, such as gums, stabilizers, and artificial additives. What we do love is real food, and when you can make a sour cream by culturing cashews to tangy, sour deliciousness, it's something to get excited about. The probiotic punch that's added to your food is a health and flavor bonus. Serve atop or stirred into any soup or stew that calls out for a dollop of dairy.

MAKES ABOUT 2 CUPS SOUR CREAM

2	cups raw, unsalted cashew pieces, soaked in water to cover for at least 4 hours or overnight, drained, and rinsed
1½	cups filtered water
½	teaspoon unrefined salt
2	teaspoons probiotic powder (see note)

In a high-speed blender, combine the cashews, water, and salt and blend until very smooth. (If you don't have a high-speed blender, you could use a food processor, but your cream will be slightly less creamy; let the processor go for about 5 minutes, stopping it a couple of times to scrape the sides and keep from overheating the machine.) Add the probiotic powder and blend just to incorporate it.

Transfer the mixture to a quart-size jar (ample room is needed for possible expansion as the sour cream ferments), cover loosely with the jar's lid, and leave in a warm part of the kitchen away from sunlight to ferment for 2 to 4 days, until it has a pleasingly sour smell to it. If you have a food dehydrator, you can speed the process along by setting it to 90°F (30°C) and fermenting the mixture in it for 12 to 14 hours. Whisk the sour cream to return it to its silky, smooth state.

Cover and store in the refrigerator, where it will keep for about 1 week.

Note: You'll find probiotic powder in the refrigerated section of the supplement section; make sure to choose a brand labeled "dairy-free" to keep your sour cream dairy free. If you have probiotic capsules, you can open a few and use them instead of going out and buying the powder.

Amaranth Crisps

These novel crackers are a delight of flavor and textures, crunchy on the outside, smooth and chewy on the inside. The tiny amaranth grains release a sticky starch when cooked that then browns to a lovely crisp when given a turn on the griddle. Serve them with a main-course soup or stew, or smeared with apple butter as a hearty snack. These crisps remain pliable, so they pack well for lunch. If there are leftovers, toast them in a toaster oven to recrisp and warm them as you would a slice of bread.

Note that the texture of cooked amaranth varies more than that of larger grains, presumably because these minute grains have considerably greater surface area. When making the recipe multiple times using the same measurement of water, sometimes the amaranth may turn out a little dry and other times more moist, but don't let this discourage you, as it's all workable. (And you'll notice the amount of liquid the amaranth is cooked in is tiny; this is because the grains will have absorbed enough water during soaking that they require only a small amount of added liquid.) If the cooked grain is dry and not cohesive, stir in about 2 tablespoons of water and simmer for an additional 2 minutes or so. If your cooked amaranth is wet, make the breads smaller to compensate for their increased delicacy.

It's well worth the extra effort to soak your grains overnight, for this step blossoms their flavor, removes their antinutrients, and makes them more digestible (see sidebar). Soaking is especially recommended for amaranth to remove its otherwise noticeably bitter flavor.

MAKES 4 (6-INCH) CRISPS

1 cup amaranth

⅓ cup stock (pages 5–10) or water

¼ teaspoon unrefined salt

Extra-virgin olive oil, or virgin coconut or red palm oil

Soak the amaranth overnight in a bowl with 2 cups of water. Strain out and discard the soaking water through an extra-fine mesh strainer, clean nylon stocking, jelly strainer bag, or nut milk bag.

Place the amaranth, stock, and salt in a small saucepan, place over high heat, and bring to a boil. Cover, reduce the heat to low, and cook for 10 to 12 minutes, until the liquid is absorbed. Remove from the heat and mix the grain from top to bottom, then cover and allow to steam for 5 to 10 minutes.

Heat a small amount of oil in an 8-inch crepe pan or skillet over medium-low heat.

With a dampened wooden spoon, remove one quarter of the amaranth and spread it onto the pan. With moistened fingertips, press it into a ⅛-inch thickness to form a 7-inch-diameter flatbread (or, alternatively, spread it to a ¼-inch thickness to form a smaller bread that will be less crisp). Cook for 5 to 8 minutes, until the bottom browns and the edges start to dry and curl up slightly, loosening the bread midway through cooking the first side. Turn the crisp and cook on the second side for 3 to 5 minutes, until browned. Remove from the skillet and repeat with the remaining amaranth, adding more oil to the pan as needed. Serve whole or broken into rustic-style pieces. Serve hot or room temperature.

Soaking Grains

Soaking is a traditional way of preparing whole grains that we regularly employ, whether the grain is part of a soup or stew or the base for serving either upon. Soaking, simply adding filtered water to cover your grains by a few inches and perhaps a splash of vinegar (any type) to help activate the grains, leaving overnight, then draining the soaking water, improves both the flavor and nutritional profile of the grains. (You can take soaking a step further by extending the time your grains spend under water to two to three days; this process, known as souring, jump-starts fermentation, and some people find this makes the grains more digestible for them.)

Soaking initiates the sprouting process, which works to blossom the flavor of the grains, and nutrition is enhanced as the antinutrients contained in the bran and hull of the grains are removed when the soaking water is discarded, making the grains more digestible and the vitamins and minerals easily accessible. An exception to the rule is wild rice; it needs no soaking, as the fermentation and scarifying processes it goes through after harvest have already removed its antinutrients.

Fermenting your grains takes a little advance planning but just a few minutes to set up. If we forgot to put the grains up last night, we might go for white rice tonight; because the bran and hull are what contain the antinutrients, soaking is not required for white rice, and in a pinch it can be the more digestible choice.

Plantain Chips

Crispy, salty, spicy, and, to our taste, a perfect accompaniment to any south-of-the-border soup, these plantain chips are a habit one can easily acquire. You'll find them more substantial than a packaged vegetable chip or cracker.

Slice your plantains as thinly as you can, using a mandoline-type slicer, if possible. Use only green plantains that are firm to the touch; if the plantain feels soft and has started to yellow, it is overly ripe.

For baking, we favor the stable fats that most healthfully withstand normal baking temperatures. Red palm oil colors the chips golden and has the least distinctive aroma, coconut oil imbues them with its flavor and aroma, and lard adds its own rich taste.

MAKES 2 CUPS CHIPS

2	green plantains (1½ pounds) scored, peeled, and thinly sliced on the diagonal
¼	cup liquid virgin coconut or red palm oil or lard (warmed if necessary to liquefy it)
1	teaspoon chili powder, or to taste
½	teaspoon unrefined salt, or to taste
	Zest and juice of 1 lime

Preheat the oven to 375°F.

In a large bowl, toss the plantain slices with the oil, chili powder, and salt and arrange them in a single layer over two rimmed baking sheets. Bake for 15 minutes, then turn them over and bake for an additional 8 to 10 minutes, until they become golden and crisp and their edges start to turn up. Transfer the chips to paper towel–lined plates and sprinkle with the lime zest and juice. Transfer to serving plates and serve, or let cool and store in an airtight container for up to 5 days.

Cornbread

When you bite into this cornbread—moist and light without being crumbly—you won't think to miss either the gluten or the dairy found in the traditional version. Try it and see whether you agree! Fine corn flour gives it a smooth texture and a double dose of coconut—both the milk and oil—give it substance while imparting just a slight coconut flavor, making this cornbread equally at home with chili or stew, dipped into soup, or drizzled with maple syrup to satisfy a sweet tooth.

MAKES 1 (10-INCH) CORNBREAD

2	tablespoons white vinegar or fresh lemon juice
1	(14-ounce) can coconut milk
2½	cups fine corn flour
1	teaspoon baking powder
1	teaspoon baking soda
½	teaspoon unrefined salt
2	large eggs
½	cup unrefined coconut oil

Preheat the oven to 375°F and position an oven rack in the middle position.

In a medium bowl, whisk the vinegar into the coconut milk and set aside for 10 minutes to sour.

In a large bowl, whisk together the corn flour, baking powder, baking soda, and salt. In a separate bowl, beat the eggs, then whisk in the soured coconut milk. Add the wet ingredients to the dry ingredients and whisk just until blended.

Put the oil in a 10-inch cast-iron skillet and place in the oven until it melts (see note). Remove the skillet from the oven and pour all but 1 tablespoon of the oil into the batter, gently whisking it in. Pour the batter into the skillet and bake for 25 to 30 minutes, until the edges start to brown and a toothpick inserted into the center comes out clean. Turn out onto a wire rack and let cool completely before slicing and serving.

Note: If your coconut oil already is liquid, pour just 1 tablespoon into the skillet; mix the rest into the batter, then proceed to pour the batter into the skillet and bake as directed above.

Almond and Flax Crackers

While the thought of making crackers from scratch may seem daunting to many of us, this recipe is in fact quite simple and doable for even a novice baker, yielding a satisfying cracker with an impressive crunch. The only challenge is avoiding overly scraggly edges when you roll the dough. But this isn't a problem: simply trim the edges and bake the scraps, too; they'll be just as tasty. Or avoid the whole issue by skipping the cutting-into-squares step, baking it all in one piece, and then breaking it into rustic-style pieces of varying shapes and sizes. For a lighter-colored cracker, use golden flax or white chia seeds.

Thanks to its almond flour and flax base and simple ingredients list, this cracker is an upgrade to going the store-bought route (many brands include starches that contain little nutrition). Serve with any of our soup or stew recipes, or as a snack topped with a nut butter or Cashew Sour Cream (page 103).

MAKES ABOUT 32 CRACKERS

½   cup almond meal

½   cup ground flax or chia seeds

1   large egg white

Unrefined salt

Preheat the oven to 325°F.

In a medium bowl, combine the almond meal and flaxseeds. Add the egg white and stir to make a dough; shape the dough into a ball, and divide the ball in half.

Put one dough mound in the center of a large piece of parchment paper and flatten slightly with your hands. Cover with a second piece of parchment and use a rolling pin to roll it out as thinly as possible; after you roll it a couple of times, gently lift the top piece of parchment, place it back down, then flip the whole thing over, lift the second piece of parchment, then continue to roll (this keeps the dough from sticking).

Put the dough setup on a baking sheet and remove the top piece of parchment. Sprinkle evenly with salt and lightly pat the salt down with your hands, then use a pizza or pastry cutter to cut the dough into 2-inch squares directly on the parchment, trimming the rough edges. Bake until lightly browned, 12 to 15 minutes (watch carefully, as the crackers can quickly go from browned to burnt), then remove from the oven and cool. Store in an airtight container for up to 2 weeks.

Griddle-Cooked Masa Harina and Daikon Flatbread

A fresh handmade tortilla hot off the griddle makes, to our taste, a most pleasing and satisfying bread. And if you've ever tried making your own, you know that it's an art to get the tortilla to inflate—and therefore steam-cook the interior. So for those of us who aren't tortilla pros, here's a great way to enjoy the inimitable flavor of masa harina. It's our improvisation of a cornmeal-daikon bread of Punjabi Sikh origin; by substituting masa harina for the cornmeal we deepen the flavor and achieve a pliable, moist bread that is cohesive rather than crumbly. With cooking, the daikon shreds become sweet, color nicely, and add texture. Best served hot, this bread is great with most any breakfast, lunch, or dinner.

MAKES 6 (5-INCH) ROUNDS

1	cup masa harina
½	teaspoon unrefined salt
1	cup finely grated daikon with its naturally forming juice
	Extra-virgin olive oil

Combine the masa harina and salt in a medium bowl. Add the daikon and, using your fingertips, blend together. The liquid from the daikon will moisten the flour enough to make a soft dough that is wet to the touch. Divide the dough into six equal portions and form each into a disk shape. Cover with plastic wrap and let rest for 5 minutes.

Take one dough disk and place it on the counter between two sheets of parchment paper. Using a rolling pin, roll into a ⅛-inch-thick round.

Heat a heavy skillet, preferably cast iron, or a griddle over medium-high heat. Add a little oil. Remove one piece of parchment paper from the round. Place uncovered side down onto the skillet with the paper still attached to the top side. Gently peel off the paper. While it cooks, roll out the second disk between the parchment paper. Cook for 3 minutes, or until the underside is flecked with brown. Turn and cook the second side for 2 minutes. Transfer to a platter. Repeat cooking the remaining disks, adding more oil to the pan as needed and rolling the next as each cooks. Cover and place in a warm oven while cooking the remaining breads if you like. Serve immediately.

Acknowledgments

How fortunate am I to play on your team, Leda Scheintaub; for your editorial expertise, friendship, and warm heart, I thank you. To our agent, Beth Shepard, for her skillful and steadfast support and for her luscious photos, thank you. To Kermit Hummel, Lisa Sacks, and the Countryman Press team, thank you.

For the unrivaled kindness of my teachers, I thank: Dzigar Kongtrul Rinpoche, Venerable Gyatrul Rinpoche, Venerable Pema Chodron, Elizabeth Mattis Namgyal, Dungse Jampal Norbu, Sangye Khandro, Ani Rioh Heigh, Lama Bruce Newman, and Lama James Kalfas.

Thanks to the peerless Mangala Shri Bhuti and Tashi Choling sanghas and especially Vern Misner, Gelong Tashi Gonpo, Ani Yeshi Dolma, Deborah J. Haynes, Peggy Markel, Paula Breymeier, Christopher Krieder, Michele DeRaismes, Basia Turzanski, Moni Banerjee, William Trione, Linda Mules Godden, Rob and Jody Wagner, Sara Scott, Brad and Tara Boucher, and the Grignon family—Dan, Sascha, and Kai.

I rejoice in my beloved children, Roanna, Jason, Eliza, and Katherine, and my exquisite grandchildren, Avram, Jonah, and Dalia.

With deep appreciation to my precious mother for her unrepayable kindnesses; how her passion for putting on a spread to feed the extended family has formed my life.

—RW

To my mentor and cherished friend, Rebecca Wood, thank you for your inspiration. And deep appreciation for our agent, Beth Shepard, for taking the concept of collaboration to a new level. Thank you to Kermit Hummel, Lisa Sacks, and Countryman Press for signing up this book.

Thanks to Liana Krissoff for copyediting the first incarnation of this book and for our friendship in food. And to friends old and new for their support and encouragement.

To my mother and father, for kvelling over me and loving my soups.

To my husband, Nash Patel; everything tastes better with you at the table.

—LS

INDEX

Note: Page references in *italics* refer to photographs.

ADDITIONAL PHOTO CREDITS